GLASGOW IN 1901

GLASGOW IN 1901

BY JAMES HAMILTON MUIR
ILLUSTRATED BY MUIRHEAD BONE
Wᵐ HODGE & CO: GLASGOW & EDINBURGH

GLASGOW IN 1901

By
JAMES HAMILTON MUIR

Illustrated by
MUIRHEAD BONE

With a new introduction by
PERILLA KINCHIN

White Cockade Publishing
2001

This edition published in 2001 by

White Cockade Publishing
71 Lonsdale Road, Oxford OX2 7ES
Tel. 01865 510411
www.whitecockade.co.uk

First published by William Hodge & Company 1901
© Text the authors' estates
© Introduction Perilla Kinchin 2001
© Map Sylvester Bone 2001

Perilla Kinchin would like to record her grateful thanks to Sylvester Bone,
for help and information from Muirhead Bone's papers; also to Jerry
Cinamon, Jolyon Hudson, Pamela Robertson and Paul Stirton.

British Library Cataloguing-in-Publication Data
A catalogue record for this book is available from the British Library.

ISBN 1 873487 09 6

Printed by Professional Book Supplies Ltd, Steventon

*Illustration opposite title page: the cover of the paperback edition of 1901,
which was printed in red and black on a buff ground. The drawing shows Gordon
Street looking east towards Buchanan Street, with the City Chambers (Municipal
Buildings) dominating the skyline.*

INTRODUCTION TO THE 2001 EDITION

'In 1901 ... "James Hamilton Muir" published such a graphic and faithful account of the city as was never seen before, and is never likely to be bettered. Glasgow in 1901 is now a classic. It is not for sale on the book barrows. It is out of print, but not out of affectionate recollection. Astute collectors will gladly pay a guinea for a reasonably clean copy.' So wrote the doyen of Glasgow letters, Neil Munro, in 1928.

One hundred years after its first enthusiastically received publication in the late summer of 1901 the book is at last available again, at a price fairly comparable with what the Glasgow publisher William Hodge originally sold it for. There was a leather-bound edition at 3s 6d, and one in paper covers at 2s 6d.[1]

Someone decided that the book should be pocket-sized, presumably with an eye to the tourist market in the year of Glasgow's second great International Exhibition. Unfortunately this does poor justice to Muirhead Bone's fine pen drawings: but while it might have been nice to start again in a more generous format, a facsimile was the only feasible option.[2] Sylvester Bone, Muirhead's grandson, has produced for this edition a simplified version of the rather scruffily drawn fold-out map of the original. We have also added at the back *The Ballade of James Hamilton Muir to his Friends*, issued on 1 January 1902, and an index to the text; while this introduction explains something about who wrote the book and what it covers.

This idiosyncratic portrait of Glasgow at its entry to the twentieth century was a memento of a special year. The death at last of Queen Victoria, who had hung on until January of 1901, seemed to confirm the end of the old era. Glasgow obviously had good partisan reasons for supporting the (logically correct and recently once more current) argument that 1 January 1901 was the real beginning of the new century: its eagerly awaited International Exhibition was opening in early May, billed as the first of the new century.[3] Paris had of course bagged the more resonant 1900 for its Exposition Universelle, which dazzled visitors with 'l'art nouveau'.

Glasgow, undisputed Second City of Empire, the Workshop of the World, was not unwilling now to challenge comparison in the competitive international arena of great exhibitions; but the foundation of the show's success was its provision to the local populace of diversion, colour and specialness, a hunger for which is expressed very clearly in *Glasgow in 1901*. The exhibition's avowed purpose of celebrating and looking back over the nineteenth century, to provide a 'resting place for pioneers' from which they might set forth into the future, made a particularly powerful story in Glasgow. The city had changed beyond recognition in the nineteenth century and was now to all appearances at the height of its prosperity and confidence, famed the world over for its ships and locomotives and manifold other industrial enterprises. This was a good time for a celebratory book.

While chauvinistic in its way, however, *Glasgow in 1901* is by no means the tourist-guide puff that might have filled the bill. It describes Glasgow's engineering and municipal achievements with real pride, but gives also a more problematic sense of the city, communicating the

INTRODUCTION

exhausting labour and the degradation of the environment that was the price paid for prosperity. The wealthy
denizens of Park Circus, in short, lived in affluence 'on the
silver lining of the clouds that hang over Govan' (p.249).

So who was 'James Hamilton Muir'? He was three ambitious young men who rose to a publishing opportunity
and put the book together in some haste. Although it was
intended to catch the tourist market they knew it would
be 'quite impossible as a guide book'[4] – it was rather 'a
pioneer attempt to break new ground in many ways', and
intended to saleable well after 1901. The youthfulness of
the authors, all in their twenties, explains much of the un-
inhibited character of the book, both high-spirited and
crusadingly serious. They are somewhat in love with the
flights of their prose – though a certain literary fruitiness
is characteristic of its period. They are keen to parade
their familiarity with lower-class 'characters' and their
entertaining command of Glasgow-speak – but this again
was currently a popular genre. For facts they are indebted of course to earlier authors – two sources are acknowledged at the front of the book; but between them they
bring into play a remarkably wide range of personal experience and interests. They have a wry and original take on
a living city; they are engaged and observant, and notably
sympathetic to the grimmer sides of Glasgow life.

This is especially true of the youngest of the three,
Muirhead Bone (1876-1953). He is acknowledged on the
title page as illustrator, but he also contributed 'Muir'
to the pseudonym, as the author of several chapters.
Muirhead was the fourth son of David Drummond Bone

(himself the son of a radical Ayr saddler known as 'Robert the Heckler'). Bone senior had come to Glasgow to work first as a compositor, then as a journalist with the *North British Daily Mail*. He brought up his numerous and subsequently distinguished brood of six boys and two girls in modest circumstances in various homes in Partick, never far from the shipyards and the West of Scotland cricket ground: he was passionate about both cricket and ships and wrote on both (the expression 'greyhounds of the Atlantic' was his coinage).

The family was not up to financing extended education and Muirhead left school at 14 to train in an architect's office. He did not last there more than four years, having decided boldly that he wanted to be an artist – though his architectural draughtsmanship was not to be wasted. With a day-job painting craft furniture for a couple of years, and then contributing drawings to various publications, he trained himself by studying paintings in the Glasgow Art Galleries, poring over prints in the Mitchell Library, taking evening classes at the old Glasgow School of Art, tramping the Glasgow streets making painstaking pen drawings, and experimenting with a copper-plate printing press he inherited when D. Y. Cameron went south. He was influenced like so many Glasgow artists by Whistler, but in his case particularly by the master's etchings. In October 1898 he wrote elatedly of a plan hatched with a group of family and friends 'to start in Glasgow a little fine-arts quarterly' entirely produced by themselves. Illustrated with original work, it was to contribute also to a literature of Glasgow, to be 'Really some attempt at adequate realization of the depths of a huge city – some adequate parallel in art to its superb life, colour, movement.'[5] Although there is no evidence that this ambitious project got off the ground, *Glasgow in 1901* was clearly related to it.

In 1899 Muirhead produced *Six Etchings of Glasgow*, and touted them around in London, a first step in establishing a reputation. In 1900 he tried opening for business as an art master in Ayr, but did not get a single pupil. But 1901 saw progress. He threw himself into the *Glasgow in 1901* project in an attempt to earn some desperately needed money, and to make his drawings more widely known. He exhibited in the Fine Art section of the Exhibition, and also produced a folio of *Exhibition Etchings*, which were produced by the well-known Glasgow photographers T. & R. Annan in their stand on site. Book and etchings were successful, and confirmed the good opinion of influential figures in the south. So it was that, despite his impassioned involvement with Glasgow, Muirhead, with a helping hand from his friend John Buchan, joined the artistic drain to London. He made the move on New Year's Day 1902.

Muirhead's subsequent career is irrelevant here perhaps, but like other Bones he made his way through application and talent, and became a leading light in the etching revival, alongside fellow Scots D. Y. Cameron and James McBey. He found his subjects now mainly in London and the south, and later in Italy and Spain, but naturally stayed in touch with family in Glasgow. A decade after *Glasgow in 1901*, probably to coincide with Glasgow's next big exhibition in 1911, he produced *Glasgow, Fifty Drawings*, lavishly published this time. In 1916 Bone became the first official war artist. He made an extremely valuable contribution to this cause, and was later involved in the foundation of the Imperial War Museum. He was a hard-working and essentially nice man, a particularly selfless supporter of many young artists, even when they would seem artistically to have nothing in common with him – Stanley Spencer, Jacob Epstein and David Bomberg were notable beneficiaries. The knighthood that crowned Bone's career in 1937 was earned by many quiet services to art.

Meanwhile, back in 1901, the deft pen drawings he produced for this book show the footings of his achievement as one of Scotland's leading draughtsmen. But the book also shows that he could write, like most of his highly literate family. In the words of his older brother, James Bone (1872-1962), the senior author of *Glasgow in 1901*, 'we were born with a pencil in our mouths'.[6] James, the second son, had also left school at 14, and worked first in the offices of the Laird Line on the waterfront: an intimacy with ships was a family thing, and two other brothers went to sea. He then joined his father as a journalist on the *North British Daily Mail*. Offered a chance in the London office of the *Manchester Guardian* he went south around the same time as Muirhead, and began what was to be a long and distinguished career with the paper, becoming its London editor from 1912 until 1945. He was made a Companion of Honour for services to journalism in 1947.

James shared his brother's artistic eye, and was a good art critic, but his forte was atmospheric descriptive writing in the urban observer mode – a literary counterpart perhaps of his brother's fascination with the city as a subject for art. James is known for other books using the formula of *Glasgow in 1901*, though more sumptuously produced: notably *Edinburgh Revisited* (1911), illustrated by Hanslip Fletcher, which was later republished as *The Perambulator in Edinburgh* in 1926 with illustrations by Ernest Lumsden; and *The London Perambulator* of 1925, illustrated by Muirhead Bone.

The third constituent of 'James Hamilton Muir', falling between the Bone brothers in age, was their friend the 27-year-old Archibald Hamilton Charteris (1874-1940). The Charteris family was another good example of talent-driven upward mobility in Glasgow, though they were a step ahead of the more bohemian Bones, having rooted into the establishment in the older generation. Charteris's grandfather was a modest but brilliant village schoolmas-ter at Wamphray whose sons had made good in the church and medicine: Archibald's uncle, Archibald Hamilton Charteris senior, was a luminary of the Church of Scotland, while his father Matthew was Professor of Materia Medica at Glasgow University. Archibald and his two younger brothers consolidated this respectable standing: Francis went into medicine, later to become Professor at St An-drews; John into the army to become a Brigadier General; while Archibald himself had chosen the law. In 1901 he had recently emerged from training as a junior with Wright, Johnston, Mackenzie & Roxburgh and in 1902 became a partner in Charteris & Hill. Like his father he was drawn to an academic career, becoming a lecturer in international law at Glasgow University between 1904 and 1920, before emigrating to a chair at Sydney University in Australia (thereby leaving behind, incidentally, the danger of impli-cation in the notorious Oscar Slater murder case).[7]

Charteris's professional West End background perhaps contributed to the wish to cloak identity with a pseudonym. His synonymous uncle, the heavyweight biblical scholar, might have been displeased to find himself identified, as he has been since in the *Dictionary of National Biography* and various library catalogues, as the author of a work of this kind, with its somewhat subversive views. While for Archibald himself to be seen dabbling as a man of letters might have undermined his professional seriousness at this fledgling stage in his legal career.

Apart from his contributions to *Glasgow in 1901*, which exploit various aspects of his background, Charteris clearly aspired to turn his late 1890s office drudgery into humorous literary sketches in the manner of the hugely popular pieces tossed off by Neil Munro in the columns of the *Glasgow Evening News*. People bought the paper avidly on Mondays to encounter a collection of matchless urban characters: Erchie, Jimmy Swan and Para Handy are the best known. Munro himself (1864-1930) was a model for the use of a pseudonym: he used the disguise of 'Hugh Foulis' for his journalism, wishing to separate this kind of writing (of which he sadly thought little, though he was its outstanding master) from his work as a serious novelist in the straight Highland romance mode.

When Charteris finally published his sketches thirty years later 'from exile' in Australia, in a book on Scottish humorous writing called *When the Scot Smiles*, he presented them archly as papers he had inherited as literary executor of 'the late J. H. Muir'. Set in solicitors' offices in West Nile Street the pieces give glimpses of city life and Glasgow characters as experienced by 'Muir', the young

INTRODUCTION

trainee. With thinly disguised autobiographical detail
Charteris claims the pseudonym as his: what the Bones
would have felt about this we do not know. If he had
thought of publishing the sketches around 1901-2, when it
seems that most of them were written, it would have been
essential to disguise his identity for professional reasons.
However, when in 1911 he wrote another piece on Glasgow
to preface Muirhead Bone's *Glasgow, Fifty Drawings*, he
used his own name.

The main advantage of the pseudonym in 1901 of course
was neatness: it covered the cracks of joint authorship,
and perhaps lent some authority to an ambitious overview
of a great city originating from three whippersnappers in
their twenties. Fortunately we know how the writing was
divided up, from annotations in Muirhead Bone's copy of
the book, supported by information in a letter.[8]

Muirhead wrote Part I, 'Glasgow of the Imagination'.
Modern taste might take time to tune in to its somewhat
poetic and elaborate style, but it is worth the effort, for
here is a truly creative attempt to evoke a working city.
Bone writes with a painter's acute sensitivity to subtleties
of colour and light, evoking the stained luminous sky re-
flecting the city's cordon of furnaces, the ever-present
haze of smoke in the streets, the reverberating clang of
the shipyards. The Clyde, dingy but 'unreasonably dear'
to natives, is at the heart of the city, and indeed of the book.
The pride common to citizens of 'no mean city' is clear,
but Bone's affection is unsentimental, and he struggles el-
oquently with the glaring environmental destruction
entailed in Glasgow's extraordinary growth and change in

the century he looks back upon. The green gardens of the
beautiful little 'Scottish Oxford' so famously admired by
visitors in the seventeenth and eighteenth centuries seem
impossible from the perspective of 'this sheer wilderness
of our own making' (p.9). Glasgow has created an ugly,
polluted wasteland for people to live in, but for all that the
city is real and alive. Thus Muirhead Bone sets out the unexpected view of the city which emerges from this book.

The greatness of the city, he says provocatively, lies not
in its much vaunted civic amenities and its well-built
streets but in its productive work. He takes the reader to
the bleak outskirts to discover a kind of frontierland,
unvisited by city man or stranger. For the real Glasgow is
to be found in 'those wonderful caves of romance, her industrial workshops' (p.11). The artist in him absorbs their
noise and flare and smoke as a setting for heroic activity,
and he uses *Glasgow in 1901* to speak solemnly of an urban
inspiration that will 'make our modern art richer than all
the old' (p.26).

He was living of course at a time of enormous artistic
creativity in Glasgow. The painters we know as the Glasgow Boys had over the last two decades earned a strong
reputation. But as Muirhead comments, their use of a
'high lyrical key of colour' seems inexplicable to one observing the drab city – and indeed they were partial to the
'kailyard' subject-matter favoured in contemporary literature, which they sought out on rural painting trips,
something which Bone had tried himself in earlier years.
Of the new generation of artist-designers developing what
we now call the 'Glasgow Style', Bone does not speak.
Their work can be read very convincingly as deriving from

[xiv]

the city but aspiring to exclude its chaos and grime through the controlled streamlined forms and meticulous colour harmonies of Glasgow's own 'new art'.[9] Charles Rennie Mackintosh and his new wife Margaret Macdonald had recently perfected an example of this in their gleaming 'white' ladies' lunch room for Miss Cranston's Ingram Street Tearooms.

Muirhead Bone as he roamed the grey workaday streets with his sketchbook was onto something more revolutionary, the challenge of developing a new aestheticism, a genuine urban art, which would capture the life of a city. A print by the Frenchman Charles Méryon opened his eyes to the artistic possibilities of scaffolding. Drawn naturally to work in black and white, Bone became the great exponent of urban building scenes, drawing structure and grandeur apparently without artistic intervention from a mass of realistic detail. In his fascination with the theme of making and remaking, he seems to carry forward the views of the charismatic Patrick Geddes, who wrote and lectured passionately at this period on the city as a living organism.[10] There was genuine if unobvious originality and modernity in Bone's work, which because it did not shock the consuming public won its way to popularity, and has perhaps therefore been undervalued.

Muirhead's introduction closes on a campaigning note: Glasgow's proud acceptance of its 'business-like' nature is all very well but for the hemmed-in lives of its working class: 'amid the blankness, uniformity, and greyness, exasperated nerves find but one outlet – in drink' (p.30). It is about time Glasgow tackled its impoverished environment; the Exhibition is a step in the right direction.

Archibald Charteris takes over to write the first three
chapters of Part II, 'Glasgow of Fact', applying his lawyer's skills to gutting various books for an account of Glasgow's early history and industry. The tale of bishops and
burghs reads rather porkily after the flights of Part I but
it turns into a useful account of the trade-based prosperity unlocked for Glasgow by Union with England in 1707.

In the nineteenth century Glasgow underwent an extraordinary transformation into a city of industries, building
upon Lanarkshire's natural resources of coal and iron ore
its mighty shipbuilding and engineering achievements.
Charteris hints however at the beginning of the end, not-
ing that in 1901 local ironstone was exhausted and cheap
iron from America was threatening invasion. Still, he says,
there is every reason to think that Clyde shipbuilders, 'like
cheap tailors', can import materials, make them up, and
export competitively again. Alas this was too optimistic.

Charteris gets into his stride in Chapter 2, giving a clear
and fascinating account of Glasgow's municipal adminis-
tration. In 1901 Glasgow was at its zenith as a 'city-state',
after the recent annexation of Hillhead and Maryhill. It
was internationally famed as an outstandingly managed
'municipal concern', and much visited by observers. As
Charteris notes, with a dig at Edinburgh, this success was
attributable to the quality of the men who had been ready
to bring their business acumen to serving the city over the
last decades. But this golden age was already on the wane,
and when he wrote again on the subject in 1911 Charteris
complained that city affairs had become so complex that
the Corporation was increasingly run by executives, while
men of quality had other things to occupy them: motor

cars had created a new class of 'half-timers' – 'city-country gentlemen'. Motors were one of the novelties showcased at the exhibition in 1901, but there is no mention of them in the book, no inkling of the enormous impact they would have on twentieth-century society.

The Council had a keen business nose for a monopoly and pursued a policy of energetic if opportunistic corporatisation of services previously provided by a virtually unregulated private sector. This section is certainly thought-provoking in the light of the reverse movement in the last two decades of the twentieth century, when efficiencies have been sought through privatisation and contracting out of every kind of public service. When Charteris was writing, the Council was on the eve of opening a municipal telephone system to compete with the National Telephone Company which had come seeking permission to lay cables under the streets. Water, gas and the tramways were previous successes, the last a particular jewel in Glasgow's crown. Since the Corporation took over the trams in 1894 fares had been reduced, and the number of passengers vastly increased; electrification, proceeding at the time of writing, was greatly boosting the service.

The first electric street lights had appeared only in 1895, but were spreading fast: 'One day the City may look garish at night.' Corporation efforts to tackle the city's slums and ameliorate some of the terrible side-effects of industrialisation are also described. The sometimes draconian measures taken to curtail infectious diseases are shocking in their own way, but had led to a marked drop in the death rate in the later part of the nineteenth century. This chapter includes some curiously fascinating detail on rates.

Charteris's third topic is the University of Glasgow, celebrating its 450th year in 1901. Writing as an alumnus and son of a professor, he gives a well-informed analysis of the strengths and weaknesses of the university. At this time about a fifth of the students were female – women had been admitted to classes in 1892. There follows a more colourful description of the typical student's life, hard-working, allegedly, but punctuated by wild larks.

James Bone brings his own background to bear in writing Chapters 4 and 5 on the Clyde and shipbuilding. He narrates the remarkable engineering feats which 'made' the Clyde during the later eighteenth and nineteenth centuries and turned Glasgow into a major port – the progressive deepening of the channel and the building of great docks. His descriptive pen comes into play evoking the sluggish foggy river, the chaos of masts and chimneys under grey skies, the whirring, pounding and clanging ... Picking up Muirhead's theme, he observes that for all its unloveliness it is a scene full of life and activity, and in glimpses of human particularity he communicates the romance of any harbour.

Shipbuilding was a source of enormous communal pride in Glasgow, and indeed the Clyde builder, 'the inspirer and pioneer', had dominated the history of the industry in the nineteenth century. But James Bone again was writing at a turning point: the loss in 1897 of the Blue Ribband of the Atlantic Challenge was still sharply felt, though Bone expresses a comfortable assurance that the Clyde would soon win it back from Germany with the five-day passage. (In fact it took another six years and government assistance before John Brown & Co. built the Lusitania to take the Ribband in 1907 – though only two years later it was snatched away by the Mauretania: one or two modifications gave the Tyneside-built Cunarder the edge over her sister ship.) At the turn of the century Glasgow was failing to meet competition with the innovations so characteristic of its earlier history. Wisps of references betray unrecognised symptoms of decline: 'somewhat overshadowed in certain respects …', 'not the cheapest …', 'despite pneumatic tools and trade unions …', the famous Clyde finish which is 'something of a fetish …' Nevertheless Bone's love of ships is infectious as he describes the huge range of vessels built so skilfully on the Clyde.

The last chapter of Part I, an astute and personal discussion of Glasgow's architecture, was written by the architecturally-trained Muirhead Bone. He contrasts the sober solid stone of Glasgow with the picturesqueness of painted London – and finds an advantage in dignity, a disadvantage in smoky dullness and monotony. The book is indeed full of passing references to factory chimneys: their disappearance and the extensive stone-cleaning programmes in the latter part of the twentieth century have transformed Glasgow's magnificent stone inheritance so that the general blackness of 1901 is hard to imagine. Bone comments favourably on recent signs of stylistic change, though a certain disdain for art nouveau is evident: a few things, he says, show 'a weedy, "arty" influence, and in certain places the strange idea seems to obtain that the vegetable is the architect's pattern' (p.140). It is not altogether clear, then, what he thought of his slightly older contemporary Mackintosh (1868-1928), today Glasgow's international cult hero, whose new School

[xix]

of Art had opened in 1899. He tends to share however the 'fevered admiration' of young professionals of the day for Glasgow's other great architectural genius, Alexander 'Greek' Thomson (1817-75).

Bone then indulges himself in detailed criticism of two public buildings intended to be crowning glories – the University buildings by George Gilbert Scott on Gilmorehill (1867-71), and William Young's opulent Municipal Buildings (1882-90) on George Square. His opinions were probably not very palatable to many readers. He makes pointed comments also on the degraded surroundings of the ancient and atmospheric cathedral, which had become marooned in the slum wilderness of the East End, crowded in by chimneys, including 'Tennant's Stalk' at St Rollox, the tallest in the world. (The cathedral's remoteness from city life and unattractive environs have remained a problem, addressed with attempts at cultural regeneration in the 1990s.) Muirhead dismisses various government buildings of the period as a story of lost opportunities. The recently completed People's Palace (1893-8) gets short shrift, mainly because of the 'trump card' which closes it on Sundays; while he describes the brand new Kelvingrove Art Galleries (1891-1901) rather nicely as 'architecture looking worried in a hundred different ways'. His full approval is reserved for progressive 'Glasgow School' projects like the enlightened purchase of Whistler's *Carlyle* for the city.

Part III, looking at Glasgow types and social habits, gives Archibald Charteris in Chapters 1 to 4 ample scope for his urban observer sketches. The tone is somewhat mannered, but these pages are full of interesting material. He writes from personal experience as an office-worker in

INTRODUCTION

Glasgow's business quarter, and focuses first on 'The City Man', 'the salt of the middle-class with all its virtues and limitations'. This is 'the plain, unassuming man' so beloved of writers of this period – active, intelligent, shrewd, practical. His counterpart at a lower level is the hardworking ambitious shopkeeper busy building a business (Thomas Lipton had been such a one). Charteris goes on to depict the deracination of those who have made their fortunes, who send their sons to English public schools and change their old ways. This is an apt personification of the complacency affecting many Glasgow businesses at the turn of the century, a loss of entrepreneurial creative thinking as second and third generations took over. In his last portrait depicting the industrial manufacturer, rarely seen on the streets, Charteris sums up the type on whom Glasgow's wealth one hundred years ago depended (p. 164 f.): 'For, were the furnaces to be shut down, or the shipyards paid off, or the factories closed, destitution would march from Parkhead to Maryhill, and would teach the merchant that the producer is more necessary to a community than a middleman.' Indeed.

The next chapter, on the Glasgow man's 'howffs', begins with an insightful discussion of the tearoom, that special feature of Glasgow life, so superior to anything found in Edinburgh or London. The phenomenon was at its zenith in 1901: as Charteris nicely puts it, 'Glasgow, in truth, is a very Tokio for tearooms.' He and the Bones belonged to just the class of city worker who found the tearooms cheap and convenient, and appreciated the distinctive new art taste of their interiors. The entrepreneurial Miss Cranston, pioneer of these civilising places and now famous as

[xxi]

Mackintosh's most loyal patron, receives her due, and the tearoom waitress gets concentrated attention too.

After discussing Glasgow's exclusive clubs, Charteris moves on to its pubs. What he has to say is notably liberal for the period, which was one of intense temperance sentiment, as the middle classes, generally speaking, sought to control working-class drinking. The Council legislated to make pubs discouragingly uncomfortable, but as Charteris says of the unfortunate working man (p.177 f.), 'A natural instinct for comradeship and brightness has driven him from a squalid home into illuminated streets, and from these the weather drives him for shelter to the public-house. 'Tis his only refuge from discomfort and weariness, and if he goes home drunk, he never meant to, and you cannot blame him.' He argues powerfully that the drink problem can only be solved by improving housing. If that is too enormous a task, pubs should become more like clubs for the poor, offering other attractions besides drinking. He even raises the idea of 'municipal public-houses', outrageous to many temperance supporters. Indeed legislation remained in force for decades prohibiting the sale of alcohol from Corporation-owned property.

In Chapter 3 Charteris speaks with the warmth of experience of the office-worker fidgeting on to 1 o'clock before he is released to the brief window of pleasure offered by Saturday afternoon (shop girls were not free until 4 p.m.). The picture of rowdy football supporters rushing by reminds us that the game was already a popular passion at this period. Charteris also evokes memorably the endless promenading in the streets which was the only leisure activity available to the majority of the working class.

Chapter 4, indebted for much of its material to James Bone, paints the Glasgow working man – intelligent, a good workman, inclined to be intractable and prickly. It is a vivid and respectful thumbnail sketch, suggesting tellingly the suppressed anger of men trapped in exhausting labour and difficult home life. Physical living conditions had improved greatly in the last decades of the nineteenth century, and education had become available to all children, but these were lives starved of real leisure or colour. Charteris well understands the importance of football as a fierce and necessary outlet, and arraigns in a way that must have shocked many readers the imposed dreariness of Sunday, the one full day allowed for 'leisure', when music and drink were forbidden, and facilities such as the People's Palace closed. Many of the traits which frightened the legislators are shown to be the fault of the conditions that ordinary working people are forced to live in.

The chapter closes with what is almost a spoof picture of the respectable Calvinistic working man of middle-class sentimental ideal: temperate, self-improving, self-disciplined. The skilled workman was indeed an important pin in maintaining industrial stability at this period, linked to his employers, whose origins often lay in this class, by an individualistic belief that a man controlled his destiny through his industry and character – an attitude which was to be dispersed by the disasters of the twentieth century. It is to Charteris's credit that he directs understanding meantime to the averagely flawed human beings who were the victims of the industrial process.

James Bone takes over to write proprietorially of quayside 'characters', drawing on his experience as a teenager working among them. After the disturbing implications of Charteris's case for social reform, this chapter presents a more remote, self-contained world, populated by stray dogs, Irishmen and Highlanders – a sidelight on the substantial immigration into Glasgow in the nineteenth century of economically disadvantaged Celts. This is a colourful parade of drop-outs and misfits to entertain yet still unsettle the respectable.

James wrote the next chapter too, giving a nicely detailed picture of the simple, somewhat dull holidays typical of the period. The loving evocation of the Highlands reflects family experience, and does not quite square with the general fashion for the Clyde resorts of Rothesay, Dunoon, and Largs. But there is a piercing sense of urban man's deprivation of countryside, and an awareness too of how mass holidaying had by this period produced 'suburbs by the sea', spoiling the very thing people hankered for. A passing reference to touring cyclists points up the book's general silence on what had been a dominating social craze of the mid 1890s, now perhaps no longer considered comment-worthy. Yachting however gets several pages.

Charteris contributes Chapter 7, on the Exhibition, taking up again his argument that the people need more provision for leisure. He makes an open appeal to the Council to spend any surplus on making life less grey for Glasgow's citizens – to do more with the parks, a magnificent civic asset, for instance, by laying on music and tearooms.

The final chapter of the book is something of a rag-bag of sketches of different streets, written as a joint effort. Muirhead takes the chance to lambast the layout of George Square, James does Buchanan Street and Argyle Street, and Charteris the sections on the West End and Glasgow's fine parks. Thus with all hands to the pump and perhaps therefore a certain amount of disarray (the last sentence is curiously lame) this quirky, intimate and affectionate portrait of the authors' native city comes to a close.

Neil Munro wrote of how re-reading the book in the late 1920s knocked 27 years off his life. It brought to mind aspects of Glasgow, details of daily life, that reminded him warmly of a different era. Glasgow had of course changed. But how much more radical is the change from our perspective, one hundred years on. 'James Hamilton Muir' looked back on a century of industrialisation. We as clearly look back from 2001 on its opposite – the de-industrialisation of Glasgow. Both have had a heavy human cost. But remarkably, considering the destruction that has been wrought, and the almost total loss of what this book sees as the fundamental heart of the city – the forges, furnaces, shipyards and docks – we have arrived a century on at something quite comparable to the confidence and pleasure in the city and its achievements that the three young authors expressed. The rest of this introduction will pass the intervening years quickly in review.

It would have been a little different perhaps if the book had indeed been republished, as apparently planned, on its 75th anniversary, in 1976. That was in retrospect another turning point: change for the better was beginning then, but was perhaps scarcely identifiable.

Similarly the terminal decline of Glasgow's heavy industries had begun before this book was written, but confidence and prosperity disguised it. However difficulties became apparent during the Edwardian years and the old stabilities reflected here succumbed to the forces unleashed by the First World War. Labour was organised at last and long-held grievances surfaced unmanageably; Clydeside turned 'Red', at least in fearful public imagination, in the 1920s. Restrictive working practices and backward-looking management styles were locked in destructive civil war, while foreign competition stole Glasgow's markets and attempts at diversification foundered. The depression of the thirties would have been a final blow, but once again war and the reconstruction after it gave Glasgow's traditional industries an unearned lease of life, distracting from attempts to develop more modern, lighter manufacturing projects. People can remember the furnace glow in the sky as late as the 1960s.

But this was the decade of continuous industrial troubles and apparently sudden fundamental change. Tennant's giant chemical works, for instance, despite having become part of ICI, finally closed; shipbuilding yards sank in rounds of hopeless expensive restructuring; shipping disappeared from the Clyde, warehouses became redundant, the Queen's Dock closed; the locomotive works in Springburn, once the largest in Europe, were demolished. The beloved trams, an urban transport system that the city would be glad to have today, were scrapped, and the motorway of the mid-sixties cut ugly gashes through sober tenement areas. Mayhem unimaginable in 1901.

Communities that had lost their raison d'être were suffering too from the mad cathartic urge after the Second World War – understandable in view of the enormity of the problems facing the authorities – to flatten the old wholesale and start again, decanting populations to the outskirts or to new 'overspill' towns remote from old roots. Living conditions were materially improved, but new problems grew up to plague the disadvantaged, now isolated in vandalised schemes and tower-blocks.

But it is easier to knock down than to build and some of the more breathtaking excesses of post-war 'comprehensive redevelopment' plans were delayed long enough by funding and other problems for the beginnings of a change of heart in the mid 1970s. But the wastelands of industrial clearances, the derelict churches and cinemas of bulldozed communities, remained dispiritingly obvious until a new willingness to work with the private sector in the 1980s began at last to reclaim some of this emptiness. The Scottish Exhibition Centre, for example, finished in 1987, was built on the filled-in Queen's Dock; while the Prince's Dock, opened not long before this book was written, in 1897, in 1988 became the site of the Glasgow Garden Festival, a modern-day if comparatively puny version of the 1901 exhibition, aiming to give out a message of rebirth and change for the better.

Things were upbeat at this point, and Glasgow's year as European City of Culture in 1990 confirmed a new cultural status. Glasgow can claim to be second only to London as a centre of the arts. Scottish Opera, Scottish Ballet and the Royal Scottish National Orchestra have their homes in the city. The School of Art has continued to train artists who win international reputations, among them chroniclers of the life of the city in a manner Muirhead Bone would have approved – just as there has been some fine writing inspired by urban realities. Museums and art galleries have multiplied beneath the umbrella of the century-old Kelvingrove. The Burrell Collection, opened in Pollok Park in 1983, shot to top Scottish tourist attraction and has symbolised Glasgow's conversion into a place which outsiders, increasing numbers of them foreign, seriously want to visit.

An emphasis on refurbishing instead of destroying, for instance in the yuppie revitalising of the 'Merchant City' in the Thatcherite 1980s, allowed Glasgow to emerge to full view as Britain's 'finest surviving Victorian city'. Its centre has remained much more complete than it might have been, as comparison with traditional rivals Birmingham, Manchester and Liverpool highlights. Care at last for the urban environment has become an important plank in the bid to rebuild Glasgow's economy on service industries, new technology and inward investment. The quality of life in Glasgow is a lure held out to relocating companies.

An examination of Muirhead Bone's drawings of course reveals plenty that has been obliterated. But this process of demolition and reconstruction after all was characteristic of the city described in this book. Indeed if the economy will only allow it there is a chance today to improve things immeasurably – especially to make better use of the Clyde frontage, which even in the glory days was not a pretty sight, and restore to the river, cleaned up as this book wanted, something of its central place in the city. The motorway, for all its ugliness, does sweep people around the city effectively, though the revitalised underground system is a more friendly asset. Muirhead Bone's key test, of whether the city is alive, is answered at one level by the unanimous response of visitors to the city's buzz. Glasgow's claim now to be Second City (Second City for retailing, that is: it lost the proper title in 1951) may seem precarious: some wonder how the cappuccino and croissant syndrome can replace the ever shrinking manufacturing base.[11] But these things are to a great extent a matter of confidence and feeling good about the city.

A century after *Glasgow in 1901*, then, a visitor arriving by train over the Clyde will emerge from the fine old Central Station into a city of designer bars and cafés, museums, and countless shops. Like J. H. Muir's stranger he or she would never venture into the outlying areas of poverty and unemployment, where many lives might seem as trapped and dreary as those described in this book, anaesthetised now by television perhaps, as much as by drink. But despite these contrasts within the city, there has remained throughout the years a strong sense of shared identity, an element of social cohesion among all classes who feel they 'belong to Glasgow'. This is a city, as *Glasgow in 1901* shows, of deep and persistent vitality, a city which commands the affection of its people and can recreate itself across the years.

NOTES

[1] Probably published in July, judging from (undated) letters. The knowledgeable but as yet unidentified author of a typescript introduction written for an evidently abortive republication of the book on its 75th anniversary, in 1976, says August. *The English Catalogue of Books, 1901-1905* (1906) says

September. It sold well and the 3s 6d edition was reissued: it is promoted on a leaflet of reviews put out by the Glasgow bookseller John Smith & Son. A letter from Muirhead Bone to Gertrude Dodd dated 13 January 1902 (he wrote 1901 by mistake) says 'Glasgow in 1901 is going well in its 2nd edition. 700 of the new 1000 disposed of already and now Hodge proposes to bring out a half-guinea edition – one bookseller offers to guarantee taking 200 himself – which is all very astonishing.' This luxury edition apparently failed to materialise.

For access to this material, permission to quote from Muirhead Bone's letters, and much help and encouragement I am very grateful to Sylvester Bone, who is currently preparing a biography of his grandfather.

[2] The original pen drawings are scattered, mainly into private collections, as Bone's work became much sought after. The Hunterian Art Gallery, University of Glasgow, and Glasgow Museums and Art Galleries collections hold a few. After some hesitation we have decided to print the 12 full-page plates, which were originally tipped into the text, on the verso of the page, with a blank on the recto, as they were in the original, though this does seem peculiar.

[3] For more about the exhibition see Perilla Kinchin & Juliet Kinchin, with Neil Baxter, *Glasgow's Great Exhibitions: 1888, 1901, 1911, 1938, 1988* (White Cockade 1988) pp.54–93.

[4] Letter dated 9 April 1901 from Muirhead Bone to Gertrude Dodd, whom he eventually married in 1903. 'Our joke is that the railway lines outside London will be strewn with them pitched away in disgust by Exhibition tourists who purchased them at the London book stalls. We propose to have a man go about picking 'em up.' The following information comes from two other undated 1901 letters.

[5] Letter dated October 98 from Muirhead Bone to Ger-

trude Dodd. The editor lined up was 'a great friend ... of mine – a man Charteris, lawyer and also an enthusiast'.

[6] Other siblings who wrote were David, later Sir David, who became Commodore Master of the Anchor Line and wrote on life at sea; John, a printer, who wrote dialect plays; and Alex, who wrote seafaring reminiscences.

[7] Archibald has been accused of involvement, along with his brother Francis, in a notorious scandal of 1907 – the murder, a bungle, of an elderly relative – for which the Jewish Oscar Slater was convicted in 1909. The case is fascinatingly explored by Thomas Toughill in *The Mystery Solved*, Canongate 1993. He argues that the establishment closed ranks round the Charteris family to pervert the course of justice. The execution of Slater was halted but he remained in prison. His case was taken up by Sir Arthur Conan Doyle, but although he was eventually released, in 1927, the case was never reopened.

[8] The copy was in the possession of Bone's daughter-in-law Mary Adshead, and seen by the writer referred to in note 1, but has unfortunately since disappeared. Corroboration in a undated letter (1901) from Muirhead Bone to Gertrude Dodd.

[9] See Juliet Kinchin, 'Mackintosh and the city', in *Charles Rennie Mackintosh*, ed. Wendy Kaplan (Glasgow Museums/Abbeville Press 1996) pp.31-63.

[10] Geddes' first major published work on urbanism was *City Development* (1904). But he had become something of a celebrity throughout Scotland in the 1890s through his high profile writings, lectures and 'Summer Meetings', and the exhibition on the city and its relation to the world at large in the Outlook Tower, an odd building in Edinburgh, 'the first sociological laboratory', from about 1892 onwards.

[11] Ian Jack wrote effectively about this back in 1984 in 'The repackaging of Glasgow', *Before the Oil Ran Out: Britain 1977–86* (Secker & Warburg 1987) pp.200-20.

[xxxi]

CLYDE SHIPBUILDERS.

GLASGOW IN 1901

By

JAMES HAMILTON MUIR

Illustrated by

MUIRHEAD BONE

Draw thy fierce streams of blinding ore,
Smite on a thousand anvils, roar
    Down to the harbour bars;
Smoulder in smoky sunsets, flare
On rainy nights, while street and square
    Lie empty to the stars.
From terrace proud to alley base
I know thee as my mother's face.
                    Alexander Smith.

GLASGOW AND EDINBURGH
WILLIAM HODGE & COMPANY
1901

NOTE

IN compiling the chapters in this book on the Corporation of Glasgow and on the development of the river Clyde, I have used freely the exhaustive work on Glasgow by Sir James Bell, Bart., and Mr. James Paton, and the various reports on the river by the late Mr. James Deas, C.E., engineer to the Clyde Trust, and by his predecessors in that office.

J. H. M.

CONTENTS

PART I

GLASGOW OF THE IMAGINATION

PART II

GLASGOW OF FACT—THE PLACE

CHAPTER I.—WHY GLASGOW FLOURISHED

PART III

GLASGOW OF FICTION—THE MAN AND HIS HAUNTS

CHAPTER I.—THE CITY MAN

CHAPTER II.—HIS HOWFFS

CHAPTER III.—SATURDAY

CHAPTER IV.—THE WORKING MAN

FULL-PAGE ILLUSTRATIONS

ILLUSTRATIONS IN THE TEXT

ILLUSTRATIONS IN THE TEXT

A map of Glasgow will be found at the end of the book

PART I

GLASGOW OF THE IMAGINATION

I

"When we came in by Glasgow town."
—*Old Ballad.*

IT must be accounted a pretty piece of stage direction on the part of the *genius loci*, that a traveller usually enters his strange city in the company of nightfall. As his train slows down and outskirts sweep out to meet him, then, whether he is entering a town of old romance, whose ancient monuments waver past him one by one like gestures of emaciated hands, or whether he finds his dark carriage " lit dreadfully " from beneath by flaring furnaces which march with him to remind him that his journey's end is an unknown black heart of the provinces—it is night, transforming all outlines and fusing all colours, that prepares the dramatic quality of his entrance.

Dusk is falling ; the train from the South is

B   [I]

The dramatic entrance. pounding on through the Black Country of Lanarkshire, past an endless procession of dour little mining villages, shot into heaps of waste rising from stagnant pools; on, past green fields blanched in the smoke, with bare little roads that scurry off to a fugitive horizon, over which the hills seem to cock their ears for a moment and sink back suddenly into the wilderness. And over the face of the land the evening sky is reeled off in an unending, monotonous ribbon by your flying train. For hours you seem to have sat in your corner, lulled by the narcotic of droning, insistent wheels, of cinders pattering on the roof of the rocking carriage pounding north-wards along the black trail. Then the fields grow rarer, then suddenly cease; suburban stations swing past with steady rows of lamps and groups of blurred people. The houses mount higher and higher on either hand; down you go into a sudden gut; out goes the last of the sunset, and descends night's curtain with a sudden run. Your train is gliding now through the squalid heart of the city; then it slackens speed, and as you yawn and collect your wraps, it rumbles out on a bridge, the darkness lifts again, and for a moment of time a vision lies before you, seen through the twinkling lattice of the girders. It is of a short reach in a river, of water coloured a faint greenish bronze, of a dusky West Highland sunset lingering overhead, where shreds of clouds are drifting into nests

[2]

for the night, of huddled silhouettes of vessels moored in mid-stream or coaling at wharves, of brown smoke and sudden lights blinking out along the quays and dulling sky and water to the mellow chiaroscuro of an old painting. For a moment it hangs before you, dreamy, yet work-a-day, instinct with the modern poetry of night fallen on unended labours. Another moment and your train rumbles over the bridge, and a swarming, nocturnal city leaps up on every hand to welcome you.

It is the Clyde you have seen, and where the faded sunset leads, is the pathway to the Hebrides. Far down, where the river becomes firth, vessels are pitching in a freshening breeze against the same late lingering sunset; lochs are sinking back into their mists for the night, and grey, weary miles of sea are heaving between Bute and Campbeltown. The " wan water " of Clyde is to the native heart inexpressibly, unreasonably dear. It is the narrow way out of toil and labour, the " world elsewhere," the casement opening on seas of adventure and romance.

This first impression may attune the stranger to much of Glasgow's life. He sees the town as a working place, hinting, in its friendly dim-ness, at a sentiment and poetry which compen-sate in a measure for the necessity that drives to laborious days. And wandering in the strange streets, his mind enjoying the pleasing zest of topo-

The "wan water" of Clyde

[3]

The town by night graphical ignorance, our traveller may continue his search for the characteristic. Before he has wandered half a mile he finds that the town is a place of hills that lift the streets in every quarter and to every angle. Hills are everywhere : the business city is deserted of its daytime workers, but the hills remain, and if our traveller would follow whither the workers have fled, it is over hills that he must take his way. The cars that make off from the centre of the city to the suburbs tell him as much in the names on their boards. And if he mounts on one that—let us say—goes westward, he will see the thing for himself. Viewed from his car-top, these hills, he will find, play quaint tricks with the night perspectives, festooning the street lamps in fantastic coilings, suspending them in mid-air like jugglers' balls, rocketing them up behind tall churches, and showering them to earth again like dropping fireworks in the far distance. A rising ground will fan reflections from the unseen lights of some street against great shadowy piles, impressive as a Roman amphitheatre. The windy, silent ways are swept and garnished ; the footlights are turned low. The few passers-by that stir on the avenues seem to him against the vague, imposing background to be intruders on the preparations for some vast spectacle. And the background itself is formed by tenements that look when lighted like palaces *en fête*, with approaches as abrupt, and mean, and

[4]

insignificant as if the buildings rose from canals. **The crescents**
Over a wide valley where he sees a river wind, **in the west**
headlands and cliffs of stone rise from the night
on either hand, approach and recede again. Now
trees appear screening the terraces, and through
them he notes the waiting carriages, warm lights
shining through open doors that mean the West
End the whole world over. He is arrested
by an almost antique beauty in the mysterious

vacant face of a grey terrace on a hill
—lit by lamps that the trees in a park screen
from his view. The river he may not discover,
nor may he guess that the faint, far-off radiance
which he observes from a hill-crest tells of ships
coaling through the night at the terminus quay,
and that the melancholy wailing that reverberates
through the air, comes from the docks. When he
thinks of return the terraces ahead are still end-

The sky

less, and he turns his back on a street running before him straight as a die, in whose distance the coloured eyes of cars beacon like lights at sea.

Throughout his wanderings the strange colour of the sky has concerned him. It is luminously tinged with a stain as of iron rust, and seems to shudder and quicken in sympathy with some unknown force lying without the city. This is the ever-present sign of Glasgow's furnace cordon. Where colour might be expected to show on the façades which the lamps illumine, he finds none; a universal greyness runs from darkness into light, and back again into darkness. And into every impression there is something cast that is dark and sombre and northern.

In the impossibility of clearing the city's embrace, and in the surprising height and massiveness everywhere, even at the verges where he would expect a gradual ebbing away into mean little huts scarcely lifting their heads above the black horizon—in all this, rather than in a grandiloquent gesture of architecture, he apprehends the greatness of the place; and in passing this judgment he is already well on the way to a true estimate of Glasgow. If he does it less than entire justice we must remember that night is on the town, and that our chimney stalks are not in view to threaten and suggest.

[6]

II

IN the pure mists of elder days in Scotland, ere **"Beloved green place"**
her sons had been called upon to endure much
"smeekiness" in the cause of her national
prosperity, the spot where our wharves and forges
now stand was a "beloved green place." The
name has that meaning, and during the long years
when we were trampling its greenness out of
sight we knew it not; yet if to-day the greenness
has gone the place remains "beloved." It is vain
to ask a native for reasons for the affection that is
in him. The affection exists, and he knows it.
Simply he cannot understand why words need
be wasted in pointing out that the hoose whaur
MacAndrew bided, and the bit green whaur he
coorted, are dearer, even more hallowed spots to
him than the burial-place of one (or all) of the
six wives of King Henry the Eighth. And it is
difficult to dispute that even the bare, grey streets
of Glasgow become in time dear as

> "—— the schoolboy spot
> We ne'er forget, though there we are forgot."

Has not the mere thought of our rainy Broomielaw brought men's hearts to their mouths while
they kicked their heels in painted lands, where
"soft lasceevious stars leered from thae velvet
skies"? Their hearts were calling for the place,
bleak, shrewd, kindly withal, place of all weathers
that end in rain, home of all trades that end in

A street in
Glasgow

furnace smoke and noise ; for the old fanfare of the
whistles as the boats cant in the river, the streets
trembling with the vibration of machinery, the

incessant clang of the riveters' hammers from **Garden Glasgow** the shipyards—all the work, strenuousness, noisiness, and grit that modern Glasgow means to her children.

That little town (the "Scottish Oxford" of a seventeenth - century traveller), white - gleaming amid green gardens on the banks of a salmon stream, with a college in its High Street, Five Stone Ports, an old Cathedral dozing on its hill overlooking the city, and with a caller air so clear "that a mountain called Ben Lomond" could be seen from their doors by the shopkeepers of King Street—this forms a reality more incredible to us than even the quaint delightful perspective we encounter in the early prints. So far have we sunk from that garden world into our darker mood and this sheer wilderness of our own making.

"There is a remedy for a' things but stark deid." And Glasgow is living, but it preys on quiet country places, hedgerows, and ploughed lands. There come times when one recoils almost in horror at this laying waste of green places where birds sang and children pic- nicked. One seems to have looked on, passive, while innocent, homely life was trampled out by the moving foot of a great city, and one's shamefacedness refuses to yield to the reflection that it was inevitable. And yet, and yet . . . either the grass must grow on the streets, or the streets on the grass. And had we preserved

Workshop Glasgow the city of our fathers, unchanged and unsullied, it had led at best a life-in-death to-day.

There is a whimsical fascination in imagining the might-have-been, our town a mild-weather St. Andrews, ourselves homing to supper under a clear, placid sky across golf-links by the Clyde, and that river itself a very sporting "hazard," where caddies might fish for the balls we foozled, and over whose shallows we might spy (in a season of clear weather) the distant roofs of Renfrew. 'Tis a pretty picture, and somehow it annoys one to know it so incompatible with the Second City of the Empire. But our fathers left us a heritage which, after all, if we consider its power and resource, was goodly enough; and, further, they left us a tradition of hard work and energy. Here James Watt, Henry Bell, and Robert Napier lived and wrought, and here in their old workshop—grown smokier and greyer— we labour to-day; cheerfully enough, too, and even a little proud of citizenship of "no mean city." So many of our days, so much of our thought, is spent here, that perhaps we endow the city with qualities by merely wishing they were there. She is the product of our middle-class virtues, with all their excellences and limitations. She does not, we must admit, traffic much in great ideals; she is practical and a little callous to what the poets have counted dear. A little careless, too, of her looks; possibly a little provincial in her love of cleanliness and con-

[10]

tempt for effect. She does not see the unconscious greatness of her pose as she stands on her hills, resting on the shaft of her hammer.

III

To understand Glasgow's most expressive contri- Pictorial bution to the picturesque, one must seek it not in her outward trappings, her charm of site, or the grace of architecture, but in those wonderful caves of romance, her industrial workshops —the shipyards, the foundries, the kilns, where strenuous figures wreathe themselves in intricate evolutions, where light prowls up and down transforming in an instant black silhouettes into sheeted ghosts, where life moves to the resonance of a clanging rhythm, and fire and steam appear in almost elemental power in the service of pigmy man. The thing surges to the eye like a giant's kaleidoscope, and no single impression remains fast in the memory. From the land where the divisions of day and night scarcely matter, one carries away again into the daylit street only a confusion of mind, a smarting in the eyes, and a singing in the ears; the blaze that held the air so triumphantly a moment ago is fallen into a heap of smouldering ashes. One can frame no words that would convey it all; it is less a series of tableaux than a sensation, or a theme out of which a painter might create visions to move his fellows. And if from these most significant characteristics of Glasgow we reluctantly turn to the picture gallery of the streets, our pedestrian muse must bear the blame. But the loss is not without its gain, for here, under the open sky, our town displays a shy beauty of its own to the man who has eyes to see and time to lie in wait upon its effects.

For him the hills are the sudden vistas in his town, with buildings grouping themselves on their tops, and people and horses on the high streets walking as on the edge of bellying clouds. The child's delight of puzzling out where he would be, if he went in at a certain door and walked straight forward, finds endless food in Glasgow. He thinks to see himself high up in mid-air, exploring, without any oddness, the smoking craters of chimneys, or climbing the delicate rigging of telegraph wires on which he had often gazed at little specks of men working, caught like flies in a spider's web. And for another delight he has the streets dipping from sight, where passers-by sink, hull down, like ships at sea, till only their heads are visible; then these, too, disappear, and the people have gone over the rim of the world. The Glasgow child running up hills to his school and tobogganing down them in the winter time becomes, in process of time, the Glasgow man who appreciates the zest of living in the garrets of the four- or five-storey tenements on the hill-

tops. How much these daily exercises improve Our hills
his health is a point we can but guess at,
lacking statistical aid. It might be said that
the Clyde is the only level highway in Glasgow.

The Panorama
and Garnethill

But more picture-like are the ranges of hills
beyond the city. For these are realities he never
puts to a proof, but only sees in the distance
from the high places of the town. Fresh and

[13]

green and bare, they loom up not so many miles away, giving to Glasgow, in their union with her grey stone, what austerity and dignity she possesses. If an uncommonly smoky street excludes the fair vision for a moment, you have but to enter any one of the parks (themselves in nearly every instance of an upland character) to become aware of them springing again into being. All the streets shedding from the northern ridges have their perspectives nobly lifted by the dim, humid hills of Renfrewshire; the north and north-west of the town look across the ancient province of Lennox—where the Roman wall of Antoninus ran—to· the rugged back of the Campsies; and of every West-End street the near Kilpatricks seem to make a *cul de sac.*

The mountain called Ben Lomond does not now, we must admit, seem so near as once it was, and if you wish to see it—in winter flushing a faint rose where the sun lies on its snow, in summer a clear turquoise blue swimming in the mist of the lesser hills—you must climb one of the little northern parks at Maryhill or Springburn, and pray, besides, for good fortune. It is from the hills about Ben Lomond that our snow comes, and winter begins for us on the first keen day of late autumn, on which we can make out their glittering table spread. A great way off from our smoke and sweat this vanguard of the Highland host stands to regard us, and to a shepherd on these hills (were it not that time and the gradualness of the change has withered his curiosity) distant Glasgow in its clouds of vapour might well seem a phenomenon as mysterious and alien to the fair valley of the Clyde as would be the presence in it of smoking, spouting geysers.

But it is not to the hills alone that one looks for a hint of picturesqueness. We defined the town as a colourless place, but, although this in

the main is true, there are reservations to be made. The nature of colour would appear in these days to be grown a puzzle as insoluble as the nature of truth itself. Our painters are found prizing the Penny Plain far above the Twopence Coloured, and somewhat to the bewilderment of the ordinary man, they bid him remark that sumptuous black, this seductive white. To them the very smoke from a chimney is " colour," and the dingy masonry, viewed through the envelope of

Nuances smoke-haze, has a "bloom" added to its tones whose quiet nuances yield a singular satisfaction to their eyes. Thus they have learned to suck pleasure even from the dark, bleak close of winter afternoons, when the rain holds off and the sun dies in a sky colourless as water, for then the monochrome of houses and squares sinks to a low, velvety blackness, as of etching-ink or of the black habit in a Velasquez, that, by its exquisite "sureness," flatters and surprises their modern sensitiveness to the charm of values. But the beauty of the black-and-white of the dull days is of a reticent kind that appears only to the trained eye. The man in the street has a simpler faith. Nothing looks "fine" save on a "fine day." So it is only when the sun comes out that he begins to look about him. And nothing short of a crimson sunset, discovering distant spires and turning nicely dark and purple the gables of his tenement (as in the oleographs at home), will draw from him the "ah" of admiration. The artist prefers his colour more in scheme, and on days of spring, which even the other concedes to be pleasant, he has a special joy, for then the gleams of sunshine sweeping over his town, as over a pale face, discover in it a kind of grace that is nearly akin to beauty. The bleak, monotonous texture of the stone vanishes, its scars and weathering not faded, indeed, but illuminated into something kindly and rare, in the fleeting caress of the gay light. The town

[16]

is wonderful in spring; out of the fresh moist **Spring days** weather leap splendid regatta days when the

ure Place

white sails endlessly over the blue. These great spectacles of sky mounting over the quiet grey

c

Dog days of our roofs seem like immense water-colours washed in by an impetuous hand which merely indicates the foreground in a few neutral tints. The dazzling face of a cloud in mid-heaven can make our stone a drab and sorry thing. Yet can that stone disclose tints that are a faithful mirror to all the weather moods. It does but lower them in key, like the reflection in some quiet pond. There is an exquisite silver moment of the town—it might be called its April mood—when the sun surprises the lingering rains, and everything, from the mud in the streets to the burnished finials of towers, gives a sudden twinkle as though by preconcerted arrangement. When the year wears on to July, and the blazing sun brings not comfort to the City toiler, but only an intolerable sense of the frowsiness of his workshop, then the dingy, colour-less streets, white-sick with smoke, appear to stand in their ranks like a sullen army of shadows intruding in the upper air in grave-clothes. In such an aspect the sun in a modern town of industry becomes a common enemy, a great irre-mediable fact—the terrible *lumière du midi* that makes foolish and disorderly the grubbings of man on the earth. The " ornaments " of his architecture, the tallest of his chimneys, his greatest railway bridges, pass unnoticed in the seething melting-pot. That great travelling white-ness, as it dissipates outlines and trivial dyes, seems to bleach the heart from sounds in the city ;

[18]

the cries of men and the grinding of machinery The sunset
sink to a low alien moaning in the ear. This is city
the light that the slums writhe under in mid-
summer.

But it is not in anger that the sun goes down.
Sunset in Glasgow is altogether gracious. It
flushes the stone with delicate washes of pink
and russet and rich Indian yellow. One blesses
the smoke haze then for mellowing and softening
the waves of light till the whole town seems a
mere golden memory of a poet's sunset architecture, like the walls of Turner's Carthage or the
palaces of Claude. Looking down West George
Street on a summer's evening, it seems to you to
hold " many-towered Camelot " at its foot. The
spire of old St. George's Church is transfigured
into a dim, sweet apparition passed from some
faded picture, its corner turrets uplifted over the
departing workers as though raised in benediction.
Higher and higher mounts the mellow flood, and
now it has ascended from the highest spire into
the sky, and all the land is steeped in the blue
depths of the twilight sea. Twilight makes of the
little strips of woodland in Botanic Gardens an
enchanted land. At this hour the little wooden
bridge over the Kelvin takes on its Watteau airs,
and one half expects to see slim little Dresden
figures in twining couples a-promenading. Come
next morning and the place of your summer night's
dream stares at you with the frigid look of a municipal park.

IV

Our milieu THE *milieu* of a town means very much more than the tale of sun or rain on its stone. It is not the fame of her towers or the beauty of her sunsets that attracts the traveller to Glasgow, and she does not take her stand on these. But wherein her character can best be seen it is a little hard to say. Perhaps our friend came nearest it when, looking in at the open door of a workshop, he was almost blinded by the smoke and iron dust, and deafened by the roar. And if he be fanciful he may think he hears, in the gasps of the exhaust pipes pushing their way through blackened roofs, toiling Glasgow drawing hard her breath. He may stroll about her streets, admiring them for their openness and height, may lounge in tea shops, amuse himself by differentiating the passing types, stand respectfully where the booming rapids of traffic converge and a policeman rules the waves, may know the insides of a few Kelvinside drawing-rooms, visit the parks, " do " Great Western Road on a fine Sunday, listen to music from the balcony of an Exhibition café, even voyage on penny steamers past the shipbuilding yards to Whiteinch—he may do this and much more than this, and yet feel that Glasgow itself has escaped him. Glasgow of " the main thoroughfares " is a pleasant place that almost deserves the laudation of the guide-books, yet it

[20]

is but the show, the result, the "agencies" (in **Glasgow from behind** the commercial sense) of the work that goes on elsewhere in obscure and un-get-at-able districts where cab-ranks are unknown. The greatness of the town is not so much an affair of well-built streets and warehouses, or municipal parks, as of creative work that transforms the iron ore brought in at one end into the machinery that throbs out at the other. The glory of Glasgow is in what the unknown "working-class districts" contain ; the crazy workshops straggling over acres of outskirts, the gaunt, blind barns that hide the smelting, forging, and casting, and squat here and there in the distant views of the town's environs that one gets from the hill-tops. The dreary wilderness of sticks along the river is the greatest architecture Glasgow possesses. The pride of the place is in its working man—the man manufacturing "in a big way," and the black squad within his gates. "Except on business," as the grimy placards at the work-gates phrase it, there are miles of out-skirts that are within the municipal boundary, shown on the map, entered in the Post Office Directory, and yet are never visited by the city man or the stranger. Enmeshed in railway net-works, girt by great dykes, on whose parapets canals wind, one only discovers them amid the chances of a resolute perambulation of the town. Here in this frontier land everything is in embryo, and here where, looking one way

Outskirts you see the country and the other way the city,
it might well be that the spirit of Glasgow would
be found. An exhilarating sense of exploration
uplifts one making such an excursion, and the
very bleakness of the treeless waste one tramps
over seems to hold something full of meaning.
The touching ugliness of so much of it readily
appeals to the imagination as something with no
reflection either in literature or art.

Under great skies, such as Michel painted,
spread miles upon miles of this landscape, inter-
sected by the roads from the town that run out
into the country and lose themselves on a wide,
disconsolate horizon, white and open roads little
frequented now, dipping out of sight and appearing again, but always wandering further away.
In the bare flats around there is something of
melancholy grandeur; one apprehends at every
turn a naked, significant beauty stripped of
embellishment; the poorhouse within its high
walls, the hospital, the prison, the works that
feed the great " crater " of Glasgow. Life is grim
here to all appearance, yet even here spring gives
a delicious shudder. There are ploughed lands,
larks ascending, men sowing, and even in season
a little reaping. There seems a tranquillity
peculiar to these lands at the back of beyond,
perhaps " the tranquillity of defeat." Man has
been content only to ear-mark this country as yet;
it struggles on, making pathetic attempts to
interest itself in its former concerns. Such places

[22]

as the Possil Marches have a wild life of their
own, and the smoke from the chemical factories
has not yet frightened away the rookeries from

Port Dundas Canal

the trees of decayed avenues. On these outskirts
one studies things without illusion. From the
flats above the canal at Port-Dundas, you examine

Sighthill the whole topography of the city from behind,
as it were, and come away with a new notion of
the relations of the districts; the fashionable
suburb in the distance is seen to be hedged in
by a district of mills and factories that draw
nearer on either side, and at your feet the gables
of tenements gape at you, with the hearths already
provided for unborn people. From here across
the plains one sees under the shadow of the
tallest chimney in the world Sighthill—a slope
from which at the beginning of last century was
descried (with the help "of a good glass") no
fewer than sixteen counties from Ben Nevis
to Fife. To-day Sighthill is a cemetery commanding no view to speak of. We are far from
picturesqueness here, and the feeling evoked by
that bare distant waste, peopled by the graves
of a hundred thousand, belongs, perhaps, to the
chastened pleasures whose cadence is music only
to a Scot. It may be he finds something of the
consolation of religion in the sight of so much
mortality. One comes to recognise it as fitting
and inevitable that here Saint Mungo's citizens
should lie to endure the sooty rain they knew so
well in life, sometimes under blackened little
patches of snow, with the day-long grinding of the
mills reverberating in the air, and a shadow
wavering across their head-stones as the smoke
sweeps out with a kind of solemnity from the
chimney tops high in the sky. Another vignette
is of the bands of workers coming home for the

night across the plains ; a mild sun sinking calm *The paysage intime*
and refulgent, and shining on their smeared faces.

These impressions constitute passages in the
great *paysage intime* of Glasgow, and out of
them might be brought a new æstheticism, such as
Raffaëlli has taken from the outskirts of Paris.
It is an old discovery that the intimate appeal
of these little bleak tracts of land whereon the
tale of man's struggles is so plainly written haunts
the mind with a suggestiveness and humanity that
may fairly be set off against the fresh beauty of
meadows and daisies.   The fascination of it all
dogs the artist while he despairs of rendering it—
the coming of morning when the new working-
day is ushered in, daybreak after a winter storm,
the streets strewn with *débris*, workmen bivouack-
ing round their fires or at work in trenches, with
the smoke of torches on their faces, street
cleaners rumbling by on their chariots, the naked
lights in kitchens and workshops, the strange
horror of men turning in the white heat of their
furnaces like Shadrach, Meshach, and Abednego,
hordes of workmen nameless and inarticulate, yet
each man at his work, a superb gesture that means
we know not what.   Though the face of Glasgow
does not yet glance at us from the walls of our
picture galleries, still the austerity, the seriousness
of great art is in her very marrow ; the provinces,
unfamed, unsung, must bide their time and their
vindication.   All views in Oxford are pretty, but
no one looks to her for painters.   Our great manu-

The treasure-
house of the
streets

facturing cities, useless for pretty views, must
come into art's province by a great portal, or not
at all.

Marie Bashkirtseff wrote of the life of the
streets as a " discovered treasure," and thought at
her death it lay in her hands. But the years spin
on and the treasure is still to find. "No artist
has yet arisen great enough to deal greatly with
the life of modern cities, but the search for that
power ever haunts the imagination of the artist
as for a new Holy Grail." We feel that in this
vineyard there lies hid the treasure that shall
make our modern art richer than all the old. It
is in the search for it that the strength of the
next generations will be expended.

V

The heart of
Scotland

GLASGOW is the largest town in Scotland—is nearly
three times larger than Edinburgh, the capital
city of the country. In Glasgow and its suburbs,
an area of (roughly) eight miles square, there is to
be found a fifth of the whole population, and this
small patch has produced two-thirds of the
country's wealth.

It is no wonder that Glasgow occupies an
exceptional position in Scotland, and is most truly
the heart of the country ; from Skye to the
Borders it drains the land to fill its workshops and
its yards. All Scotland looks to Glasgow as the

field for employment and energy. Edinburgh the
Scots rustic remembers as a place of a castle with
military kilted lads, of memories of the Black
Watch, where old Scots tradition flares out splendidly on a "Hogmanay" night with old Scots
drink and currant buns—a town so purely Scottish
as to seem cut off entirely from the world at large.
But Glasgow is the place for his advancement—
the focus of his interest and thought—for are not
Donald and Angus employed there, and is not
young Archie going to enter a shop there when he
is old enough to leave the little stony farm of his
fathers? The high buildings, the very number of
the public-houses, the "bleezing lowes" one after
another along the railway line that ushers him into
Glasgow intimidate his simple mind like the
entrance to a great house. His country newspaper
is full of the doings of Glasgow; he has acquired
unconsciously the habit of looking to her to do the
great things for Scotland. This is "Glasgow's
Exhibition," therefore it is worth taking one of
the few journeys of his lifetime to see it. The
charm of Edinburgh—the flavour of the distinguished something in it—its ancient architecture
and beauty of site, even its clearer air,
fails to arouse in him any enthusiasm,
for the Glasgow Colosseum is finer to a
countryman than all the old mansions of
the Lothians, and Edinburgh Castle does not
impress him like the electric cars of Glasgow.
More than Edinburgh's charm, it sticks in his

The candid mind that things are done closely, not to say
friend "scrimpit," there; while here is a perfectly
marvellous profusion of siller and of sights that
can be seen for nothing. But when Glasgow has
Archie and Donald in her keeping, and the work-
gates and the shop doors bar them from the
liberty of the streets, she keeps their honest noses
hard at the grindstone, and when their laborious
day is over, she gives them the key of the murky,
nocturnal town spreading over treeless wastes, or
for refuge the shelter of her 1404 taverns.

Our traveller, however, to whom our electric
cars and crowded streets are matters for criticism
and comparison rather than respectful admiration,
finds Glasgow merely one more of the middle-class
manufacturing centres, and very likely her contempt for "effect" and apparent devotion to
gross materialism appears to him sometimes in a
mean light. It is a perpetual astonishment to
our visitors to find that Glasgow painters form
the only serious group of painters in the provinces.
Their pictures, often attuned to a high lyrical key
of colour, seem to our visitors inexplicable if considered as manifestations of our city—so utterly
divorced appear the lives of its inhabitants from
poetry and the vision splendid. And the heavy,
ugly, and provincial side of Glasgow cannot well
be ignored. Considering the situation of the town
there are few traces anywhere of decoration or
ornament adequate to its opportunities. Frankly,
Glasgow seems a thriving city, but as little as

[28]

Manchester or Liverpool does it look the
"Second City of the Empire." "Business-like"
—this to your true Glasgow man is the
sum of all the virtues, and, holding it,
he believes he has draped his multitude
of sins. He does not mind in the least—
indeed, he rather enjoys—the reproach you bring
against him of a polluted Clyde; it suits his
sardonic humour to regard it as but one more
proof of how very "business-like" he has made
things. He believes in the picturesque in its
proper place, but not in Glasgow, which he will
tell you is a workshop. But he does not seem
alive to the fact that in its grimy midst
his workpeople, willy-nilly, must make their
dwelling-place and spend their lives, their leisure
as well as their working hours. If only his workpeople might have their homes miles away from
the workshop smoke, and in houses with a little
elbow-room, not packed, as they are here, fifty
or sixty to one common stair—then he might be
justified.

As it is, our Glasgow man must, we fear, be
judged to be cynically indifferent to the obligations which he owes to the place that yields him
his money; two polluted rivers, the Clyde and
Kelvin, cry out against him; no trees are
planted on *his* streets. "Things should be done
well"—he does not grudge what time or money
he spends on them. They have been done
well — rigidly, properly, and decently — his

[29]

Grim Glasgow conscience is easy, is not *his* the "model municipality"? But the grace of life is somewhat laggard in appearing also in "model" proportions. The water is good, the gas is good, the drainage system excellent, the Corporation tramways admirable; yet somehow or other the long northern day is somewhat dreary to the toiling thousands in this vast city. A wet Saturday night in winter finds it so; "the heavy sleep of the provinces" becomes a nightmare then to a sensitive soul; whole districts hold a monstrous carnival of drink and misery. Deep down the old terrible *perfervidum ingenium Scotorum* lives on, and amid the blankness, uniformity, and greyness, exasperated nerves find but one outlet—in drink. One hesitates to say that Glasgow is ahead of any other of the great provincial towns in solving the problem of how the life of its workers may be made a little more gracious and tolerable and sweet. Yet in this year 1901 there are not wanting signs that the "second vial" of Glasgow's conscience—the duty it owes to the seemly life—is about to be opened. What is the Exhibition but her *amende honorable?* For six months her citizens are joint hosts in the great guest-house at Kelvingrove. It *had* to come—Glasgow's handsome settlement of her heavy overdrafts on the hospitality of Scotland and the world at large. That the Exhibition will leave behind it a humanising influence we know. It will hasten the coming of our clean rivers, our flowers and trees, and help

[30]

to rend that intolerable blanket of smoke which, The amende honorable while it keeps out the sun, is not even proof against rain. We want some "niceness" in the conditions of our citizens' lives, and justice done to our city's looks that we may love her in the sight of men as we have loved her shamefacedly and in secret, from the dumb instinct that bids man respect the wrinkled hand that feeds and clothes him and finds him shelter.

"Glasgow is the centre of the intelligence of England."

Grand Duke Alexis of Russia, 1880.

Campsie Hills
from Kelvingrove Park

PART II

GLASGOW OF FACT—THE PLACE

I

Why Glasgow Flourished

So intimate in the early days were the Church's relations with Glasgow that had the City really taken for its motto, "Lord, let Glasgow flourish by the preaching of Thy word," none could well have cavilled at the choice. St. Kentigern, a worker of miracles (come from Culross), discovered in 550 A.D. a hamlet on the banks of the Molendinar Burn, and as Bishop of the See erected there the church which in the early part of the thirteenth century his successor in the See rebuilt as the Cathedral of Glasgow. Bishop Jocelin obtained for the City its first form of government and first trading privileges, securing in 1176 its erection into a burgh of bishop, with a grant of a weekly market, and in 1190 the right of holding a yearly fair. To Bishop Turnbull it owed, in 1450, its erection into a burgh of regality and the foundation of its University. Yet the City's obligations to its

Glasgow and the Church

D

Glasgow a
Royal Burgh

bishops were perhaps more than balanced by the bishops' powers over the City. The charters from the King were taken in their name, and they were beyond doubt the temporal rulers of the town. From 1476 they had "power to appoint and dismiss provosts, bailies, sergeants, and other officers as may seem to them expedient for the government of the City." And not even the Reformation, which turned Glasgow into a hotbed of Protestantism, destroyed this power at once; for after Archbishop James Beaton, in 1559, had fled to France, taking with him, among other things, the University mace (now recovered), James VI., in 1600, invested the Duke of Lennox in the bailiary and justiciary of the Barony and Regality of Glasgow, with all heritable rights and privileges hitherto held by the archbishops. And though in 1636 a charter of Charles I. recognised the City as one which his predecessors had erected into "ane entire royal burgh," it was not until 1690 that, by virtue of an Act of Parliament confirming a charter of William and Mary, the last restrictions on the freedom of the royal burgh were removed. Henceforward Glasgow might choose her own magistrates "as fully and freely in all respects as the city of Edinburgh, or any other royal burgh within the kingdom." The City was rid of the Church, and with her motto curtailed to "Let Glasgow Flourish," she was looking forward, forgetting past benefits.

This liberation was achieved almost within sight of the Act of Union of 1707, which was to furnish the opportunity of the City's subsequent rise to greatness. Yet none foresaw these effects of the Union, and in a country which, even by the standard of the time, was miserably poor, the prospect of subjection to English taxes and English Customs duties made this measure hugely unpopular. It was denounced from pulpits and in meetings, and Glasgow was the scene of a furious anti-Union riot, which probably expressed the popular sentiment of the nation regarding this annexation to a foreign kingdom, which was to extinguish Scots independence, Scots trade, and all that made Scotland distinctive. The results were, of course, quite different, and J. R. Green was simply accurate when he said that " to Scotland the Union opened up new avenues of wealth which the energy of the people turned to wonderful account. The farms of Lothian have become models of agricultural skill. A fishing town on the Clyde has grown into the rich and prosperous Glasgow."

But no wonder she was only a fishing town. Her geographical position forbade her to be more. It is true she had access to the sea—to the Atlantic Ocean—but with the trade of Europe setting eastward this was a small advantage. In fact, as Sir Walter has pointed out, she lay on the wrong side of the island. But when America was made the goal of traders, her time came. She ceased to be

Early trade   as remote as St. Kilda, and became a starting-point for maritime enterprises. And the liberty to use her new opportunities came with the Union. Nor was she wholly unprepared, for she had already made a beginning in commerce, adventuring, as we shall see, even to France. Herring and salmon had been her first staple export, and so greatly had this trade thriven that 1700 lasts, or 20,000 barrels, of cured herrings had been shipped in 1564 to Rochelle alone, and in the beginning of the sixteenth century nine hundred boats were fishing in the Firth of Clyde above the Cloch. By the middle of that century her trade was not inconsiderable for the time. In 1656 Tucker, the commissioner of Oliver Cromwell, reported that all her inhabitants were traders—" some to Ireland with small smiddy coal, carried in little vessels of four to ten tons burden; others to France with plaidings, coal, and herrings, from which the return is salt, pepper, raisins, and prunes; others, again, to Norway for timber "; while every one trades " with their neighbours the Highlanders," who in summer come from the islands round the Mull of Cantyre, and in winter cross at Tarbet into Loch Fyne, bringing " pladding, dry hides, goate, kid, and deere skins," and carrying away the goods which the merchants of Glasgow offered for their wants. Some traders even adventured to the Barbadoes, but with doubtful success. Twelve vessels of a total tonnage of 957 were owned in the City, but never came up to the port owing to the shallowness of the river " every day mineasing and filling up." In 1692 the Commissioners of the Convention of Burghs found that the export and import trade was of an annual value of £17,083 6s. 8d. sterling, and that the City merchants owned fifteen vessels, measuring 1182 tons, of a total value of £3877 15s. 6⅜d. sterling, but the trade was in decay, and many of the best houses in the City were unoccupied.

Then came the luckless Darien scheme, to which £400,000 had been subscribed, and which in July, 1698, sent out 1200 picked men in three small vessels to found on the Isthmus of Darien a Scots settlement which should rival the wealthy colonies of England in the New World. And when in 1700 the news came that—thanks to the enmity of the English Government and the active hostility of the Spaniards—the daring venture had failed, Scotland, and Glasgow with it, was all but overwhelmed in bankruptcy. Not until 1717 did a Glasgow vessel again adventure across the Atlantic Ocean. But when it did so, new conditions prevailed. The Union had been accomplished, and the vexatious Navigation Laws, which had prohibited Scots vessels from trading to the English colonies and from carrying cargoes from an English port unless two-thirds of their crews were English-born, had been removed for ever. And from that time onwards Glasgow merchants began to exploit their new opportunities, at first in a tentative fashion, but afterwards more briskly as the profits of their

foreign trade became more apparent. And even
in 1727 Defoe was so impressed by what he saw of
Glasgow and her commerce that his account seems
to the modern Briton not unlike an alarm cry at
the magnitude of foreign commercial competition.
So detailed and interesting is it that we give it
almost in his own words. "The town," he says,
" has the face of foreign as well as domestic trade ;
nay, I may say 'tis the only city in Scotland at
this time that apparently increases in both .   .   .
for they now send near fifty ships of sail every year
to Virginia, New England, and other colonies in
America." This foreign trade he finds to enjoy
many advantages. The merchants " can furnish
not only what they have in sufficient quantities,
but some in greater perfection than in England
itself.

1. "They have woollen manufactures of their
own, such as Stirling serges, Musselburgh stuffs,
Aberdeen stockens, Edinburgh shalloons, blankets,
etc.

2. "The trade with England being open, they
have now all the Manchester, Sheffield, and Birmingham wares, and likewise the cloth, kerseys,
half-thicks, duffels, stockens, and coarse manufactures of the North of England brought as cheap, or
cheaper, to them by pack-horses as they are carried
to London, it being a less distance.

3. "They have linens of most kinds, especially
diapers and table-linen, damasks, and many other
sorts not known to England, and cheaper than
these, because made at their own doors.

4. "What linens they want from Holland or Hamburgh they import from thence as cheap as the English can do, and for muslins their own are very acceptable, and cheaper than in England.

5. "Gloves they make better and cheaper than in England, for they send great quantities thither." Nor are they limited to their own local market for obtaining " a vend and consumption " of the goods which their vessels bring from America, since " they have lately set up a wharf at Alloway, on the Forth, whence they trade with Holland, Hamburgh, and London." Finally, there is pointed out an advantage in favour of Glasgow which might well have stood at the beginning of his account. This is the advantage of geographical position. Not only is the northern port from fourteen to twenty days nearer Virginia than is London, but the Scots ships being quickly on the high seas are free from " privateers, which throng the channel in time of war, and force ships to wait to go in fleets for fear of enemies." Glasgow, you see, is no longer on the wrong side of the island, but is a point of departure for maritime adventures.

The trade with America, which Defoe describes, increased during the eighteenth century to a great volume, and formed the origin of Glasgow's wealth. In particular, the tobacco trade so throve that when the American war broke out Glasgow was the main emporium for tobacco in Europe. "In 1772 the following quantities of tobacco were imported into the Clyde:—From Virginia, 33,986,403 lbs. ; from

Tobacco trade North Carolina, 755,458 lbs.; from Maryland, 11,313,278 lbs.; and in the same year, besides considerable quantities sent to Norway and Denmark, there were exported from Glasgow to France 20,744,943 lbs., Holland 14,932,543 lbs., Italy 311,707 lbs., Germany 3,868,027 lbs." (Strang's "Glasgow and its Clubs.") Thirty-eight firms were engaged in the trade, and made extremely handsome profits, for the system of business conduced to that result. The merchants who supplied the goods to the adventurer were not paid until his ship had returned from America some eighteen months later, and her cargo of tobacco had been sold. In this way the adventurer reaped most of the profits and had the benefit of trading on credit of other people. To these latter persons it must have had its ironic side to see that the " tobacco lords " regarded themselves as very little lower than the angels, and quite a great way above the profane vulgar. They wore a distinctive dress of scarlet cloaks, curled wigs, cocked hats, and gold-headed canes. The " Plainstanes " (the pavement in front of the Tontine) was their own appointed country, where none might speak to them until he had been first addressed. They were, indeed, " most superior persons."

But their evil day came with the American war, which ended their trade. So keenly did the rebellion affect Glasgow that she raised 1000 men at a cost of £10,000, and fitted out no less than fourteen privateers to fight for her Markets and

her King. But though the war killed her tobacco
trade, it proved to Glasgow a blessing in disguise,
for Gibson, a shrewd merchant, writing in 1776,
points out that whereas the adventurers to America
had been content to wait eighteen months for their
profits, they now, by force of circumstances, found
markets which yielded them a return in six months.
And in the nineteenth century they were to find
quite new fields for activity.

In the nineteenth century Glasgow has
been turned by the so-called Industrial Revolution into a city of industries. The
phenomena were of the usual kind. The
means of communication were multiplied;
even the old century saw, in 1790, the completion of the Forth and Clyde Canal, which had
been begun in 1768; and in the early part of the
new the first of the railways, which were to cover
central Scotland with a network of iron, was laid
between Kilmarnock and Troon. And as we shall
see in detail later on, the Clyde was changed from
a salmon river into a tidal canal, to lead as by a
highway to prosperity. In 1801 Tennant founded
the chemical industry in Glasgow by establishing
at St. Rollox the famous works for the manufac-
ture of solid bleaching powder, and other products
of alkali industry. To-day the highest chimney
in the world marks the site, and enjoys at the top
purer air than it allows to the works about the
base. In 1811, Henry Bell, of Helensburgh,
making use of James Watt's improvements on the

Industrial beginnings

[41]

Mineral industries steam engine, designed the engines of the "Comet,"
which in the following year began, as the pioneer
of steam navigation, to ply between Glasgow,
Greenock and Helensburgh. And, chief cause of
all, the mineral wealth of Lanarkshire underwent
exploitation. Coal had been worked from early
times—in the Barony of Glasgow since the end of
the sixteenth century—and iron had been manu-
factured since the foundation of the Clyde Iron
Works in 1782. But when Mushet in 1801 discovered the black-band ironstone, of which Lanarkshire had immense deposits, and J. B. Neilson, the
engineer to the Glasgow Gas Works, in 1828
invented the hot-blast process of smelting (by
which Mushet's discovery could be turned to
account), the iron and coal industries received an
immense stimulus. And on their prosperity Glasgow rose to greatness. With coal at her doors she
became a centre of manufactures, and her iron
supply made her a headquarters of all engineering
industries. The river, too, was a factor of
supreme importance, for on its banks shipbuilding, which the local abundance of iron and
steel made possible, flourished and became the
most famous industry of Glasgow. Boiler-making
and marine engineering sprang up also, and the
three industries have produced, as their counterpart in the animal kingdom, the man M'Andrew,
known in every seaport from Port-Glasgow to
Shanghai as the Clyde-trained engineer, and
recognised by a selecter public as the inspiration
of a Hymn.

Coal mining and the iron and steel industries
of Lanarkshire remain the rock on which the
prosperity of the city is founded. But the
foundation will not last for ever. The local
deposits of iron ore are already exhausted, and
Spain, in return for coal, at present makes good
the deficiency. An iron invasion is threatened
from America, which is to crush the Scottish
foundries out of existence. Yet even if this pass
should be reached, the shipbuilding industry
might still greatly flourish. For the builder is a
business man first and patriot afterwards. And
if American materials are cheaper (which is the
condition of their success in our markets), he
may use them instead of native products. In that
case America might find herself exporting plates
to Clyde builders, who, like cheap tailors, would
make them up into ships and return them at a
price impossible on the other side of the Atlantic.
But these things are in the lap of the gods.
What we know at present is that the Clyde industries go on with vigour and success, and that
steel rails and whisky still form the " Glasgow
cargo " of clippers outward bound to Australia.

Of the position which she has attained through
this prosperity Glasgow is justly proud. She
claims to be the Second City of the Empire, as she
is undoubtedly the first in Scotland for population,
trade, industries, and wealth. She is not merely
a home of manufactures, but a seaport and a
centre of trade. Her river and her railways,

[43]

Trading
capital of
Scotland

giving access the one to the ocean, the other to every British town, have made her the main centre of distribution north of the Tweed. Moreover, she is the Model Municipality, a shining example of the benefits conferred on her by a union of public spirit with capacity for affairs. She is the Trading Capital of Scotland. In a local way she is even a metropolis, for she is the base of supply for the West and South-West, for the Highlands and Hebrides, and therefore the goal of all restless folk in these districts. Also she is the seat of an ancient University; and thus she never wants for immigrants, some seeking fortune, some learning, some (more simply) work. If luck favours, she sees them settle within her bounds, multiply and add daily to her wealth and greatness. In time, too, she finds them or their offspring grown into Glasgow men and indistinguishable (except to experts) from her native-born.

II

Her Model Municipality

IF Bailie Nicol Jarvie were to come stepping along the Trongate and "up by" to the Corporation Buildings where his successors in office perform their functions, who could blame him if, like Mr. Johnston in Stevenson's poem, he "scunnered at the new precentor "? His bonnie town of four square streets swollen into a shapeless wilderness of buildings overhung with smoke and full of strange life and noises! His very Saltmarket

Saltmarket

rebuilt, in part in tasteless red, by no others than the Councillors themselves, and tenanted— mark you—by foreigners, policemen from the Highlands! And these same Councillors bringing water from Rob Roy's country, and driving the herring out of the Clyde, and burning the town's

[45]

refuse, and whitewashing houses, and lighting
the streets after elders' hours, and deepening
the Clyde, and allowing Corporation cars to run
on the Sabbath Day, and—" Ma conscience, sirs,
but it's a sair declension frae the auld ! An' I'll
awa hame ! " In truth, the change is staggering,
even in the matter of figures. The population
of the town in the good Bailie's day was some
18,000, now it is over 750,000. The rental,
though the exact figures are lacking, was perhaps
£15,000 ; now it is £4,499,520, having increased
in the last thirty years by 130 per cent., and
is paid by 182,041 occupiers. The City's assets
now amount to thirteen and a half millions of
pounds, her liabilities to nearly ten millions.
The year's revenue is close on two and a half
millions, of which two and a third millions meets
the year's expenditure.

It is still the Town Council which administers
the City's affairs. But the functions of that
body have been changed out of recognition. No longer does it merely rule, to
maintain order and protect property within
the bounds, but it now renders services to
the citizens which they cannot render to themselves or to each other, and exacts from them
the performance of certain duties whose sanction
is the public interest of the community. And
the general result seems, without exaggeration,
to be that the modern City is reverting in importance to the position of the City-state in classical

antiquity. In the particular instance before us The Council
this change and the process of the suns have and the
brought great fame to Glasgow and its adminis-
tration, not in Britain only, but abroad. We
are even told that in America she is praised as
the best-managed "municipal concern" on earth,
since her expenses are met out of the profits
from her private enterprises. The praise being
no more than due brings no blushes to our cheek,
but the reason for it is not so. Yet only dull,
short-sighted people regard municipal rates as
imposts. They are payments for services ren-
dered, the price of our blessings. Nevertheless,
they shall not be revealed until we have the
reader rooted and grounded in admiration for our
municipality.

After all, the wonder is less that the Corporation serves the City well, than that the citizens
do not serve the City better. Your municipal
voter is apathetic at election times, and deserves
little credit if the Town Council is generally
recruited from the right men. It may be that
in a city like Glasgow, where the typical citizen
is a man of business, the Town Council is his
natural goal if he has public spirit and finds
in his calling less than full scope for his activities
and ambitions. In Edinburgh, on the other
hand, the citizen who counts is the professional
or *quasi*-professional man, and when the Town
Council calls him, he passes by on the other side,
not daring to seek eminence outside his pro-

fession. His municipal duties he performs in
payment of rates, and perhaps in ungrudging
voluntary criticism. "Municipal honours" he
leaves to those who, by an inch or a mile, have
missed being in the right set or the right calling,
and need some stairway out of the ruck. But
in Glasgow it is only a small and (believe us)
most highly-bred and wealthy minority who
would feel that they had betrayed their caste in
entering the Council. And thus by a kind of
social gravitation the right man filters through
the apathy-bed into the Council. Once a member, he finds his business ability more in demand
than his ideas, if he has them. It would be
unfair to say of that body, as Heine said of
Göttingen, that quarantine is imposed for some
decades on new ideas to prevent speculative
smuggling. For the Council follows a clear
policy. As an elected body, it does not pre-
tend to be much in advance of the common
opinion of the electors, nor is it a pioneer. Yet
any reasonable, practicable measure or undertaking which the citizens insist upon, it will
adopt. But where the rendering of some service,
necessary to the community, involves the use of
its property, and is either actually or potentially
a monopoly, it intervenes to undertake that
service. The most recent application of this
principle was made in dealing with a request by
the National Telephone Company for permission
to lay their telephone wires under the streets,

which are the property of the Corporation. The request was refused, and the Corporation are now on the eve of inaugurating a Municipal Telephone System to compete with the Company's, whose annual charge shall be half that of the Company's. In the Corporation management of water, gas, and tramways you have the same principle applied in other and older instances.

For municipal purposes the City, which, like London, is an Administrative County, is divided into five-and-twenty wards, from each of which the qualified ratepayers (men and women) elect three members to the Council. That body, with two *ex officio* members, the Deacon-Convener of the Trades House and the Lord Dean of Guild (the president of the Court charged with the supervision of buildings in the City), therefore numbers seventy-seven members. At the head of it is the Lord Provost, who, if zealous in his office, is the hardest worked man in the city. He is its First Magistrate, and may be Lord Lieutenant of the Administrative County. *Ex officio*, he is member of each of the ten committees of the Council, Chairman of the Clyde Navigation Trust, and member of the University Court. And, by courtesy, he is entitled to a seat on every Board to which the Council sends a representative. With the gift of words, he is the Public Orator of the City, opens most of the bazaars, presides at nearly all the charitable

(marginal note: The administrative system)

E

The Town Council

concerts, raises funds for the relief of distress in all places nearer than Mars, entertains selected companies of the citizens, and at odd moments attends to the business which provides his private income. At the end of his three years' term of office he is usually made a baronet or knight, having earned his reward. His prominent fellow-officials are the fourteen Bailies, who preside in turns at the Police Courts of the city, the City Treasurer (unpaid), who is convener of the Finance Committee, the Town-clerk, and the City Chamberlain (the actual Treasurer), both salaried officials. The Council meets for the despatch of business every second Thursday in the Corporation Buildings in George Square, and committees and sub-committees meet there every day and all day long. And its activities are varied enough. The Police Department is charged with the policing of the city, " with the lighting of the streets, lanes, courts, and stair-cases of the City, the paving of the streets, the providing of drains and sewers, and the cleansing of the City." And there are departments which provide the City with Gas and Electric Light, Water, and Tramways. Also, there are committees not only for the important matter of Finance, but for the Bazaars, Halls, Clocks and Bells, for the Churches and Churchyards owned or maintained by the City, for the Mitchell Reference Library, for the seventeen City Parks and Gardens, for Picture Galleries, and Museums. As the most tangible services which the Corporation **The water** renders to its citizens are in the supply of water, **supply** gas, and tramways, we may give in some detail an account of these undertakings.

In point of age and importance, the water

Mitchell Library

supply comes first. When the wells and springs which supplied Glasgow until the beginning of this century were found insufficient for the needs of the population, the most obvious source of supply was the Clyde, and accordingly it was

Early sources of the supply from the river that in 1806 the Glasgow Water Company was empowered to draw water to supply the City and suburbs. James Watt was one of the engineers, and on his advice the water was allowed to filter itself by passing through the sandy banks of the Clyde at Dalmarnock, two miles above Glasgow Bridge, and was collected in culverts placed below the level of the river on the south side, and then carried in a spherical jointed pipe of Watt's invention under the river to the north side, and thence pumped to the consumers. Two years later (1808) a second company (the Company of the Proprietors of Cranstonhill Water Works) obtained powers to draw water from the Clyde at Anderston, a mile below Glasgow Bridge, to supply Cranstonhill and the western suburbs. But this company did not prosper. At Anderston the Clyde, less pure than at Dalmarnock, was daily becoming fouler. The company was therefore forced ultimately to obtain its supply from Dalmarnock also, and the great cost of pumping the water westwards into the company's own territory made profits hopeless. In 1838 the two companies were amalgamated under the name of the Glasgow Water Company, and continued for many years without opposition to supply the city with fairly bad water to an extent of 26 gallons per head of population per day. As early as 1845 a rival scheme of procuring water from Loch Katrine, the present source, was projected, but was withdrawn on the

Company undertaking to tap Loch Lubnaig, a source still more distant. But though powers were obtained, the difficulties of providing the necessary compensation water for the river Teith, which drained Loch Lubnaig, proved insuperable. In 1848 another company, the Gorbals Water Company, obtained powers to supply the Gorbals and other places on the south of the river with water drawn from the Brock and its tributaries in Renfrewshire, and provided a water so superior to filtered Clyde water that the revenue of this Company very speedily reduced that of its older rival. At this time, as the joint supply amounted to 30 gallons per head of a population of 400,000, the complaint was not of the amount but of the quality of the main source of the supply. The Clyde even at Dalmarnock, above the centre of the City, was becoming disgracefully foul, and it was no wonder that the old scheme of tapping Loch Katrine became popular. In 1854 the Corporation introduced a Bill into Parliament which was rejected mainly because the Lords Commissioners of the Admiralty intervened in the interests of the Navigation Trustees of the Forth, and averred that the diversion of so much water from the drainage area of the Forth would presently render that sluggish river unnavigable by reason of silting. In the following year the Corporation had no difficulty in disproving this contention, and received power to buy out the existing Water Companies and provide a municipal supply from Loch Katrine. The source, the

Loch Katrine Water Works

Loch Katrine Water Works experts advised, was the best in Scotland. The Loch is the principal drainage basin of a district perhaps the wettest north of the Tweed, with a mean annual rainfall of 92 inches, rising, in very wet seasons, to 130 inches. The water is remarkably uniform in quality, temperature, and colour, and beyond straining, to keep fish, leaves, etc., out of the consumers' bath, requires no treatment at all. Further, it is very soft, and on this account alone Mr. Bateman, the Corporation's engineer, estimated in 1855 that the annual saving in soap to

Victoria Park

the inhabitants of Glasgow would amount to £30,000. Under this Act the Corporation was empowered to raise the level of Loch Katrine four feet above the summer level, and to connect the Loch with the City by means of pipes. The works were completed in 1859, and on 14th October of that year the water was turned on at Loch Katrine by Her Majesty Queen Victoria. In March of the following year the public supply was inaugurated at a first cost of £920,000. Since then, notably in 1864, 1868, 1875, and 1877, various improvements and additions were made to the system, and in

54]

1880 the whole length of pipes of 36 inches in gauge and upwards amounted to more than $44\frac{1}{2}$ miles, and to the same date the total cost was £1,454,000. Present capacity of works

In 1885 the increase of the consumption of water in the City made it necessary to extend the area from which the supply was drawn. Accordingly, in that year Parliamentary powers were obtained to raise Loch Katrine by five feet more, to drain to a depth of three feet below summer level, and to lay Loch Arklet (which drains into Loch Katrine) under contribution. Powers were also taken to duplicate the entire waterworks of the City. The effect is to give the Loch Katrine works an ultimate reservoir capacity of 12,000 million gallons, which, with the Gorbals capacity of 1058 millions, gives a grand total of, roughly, 13,000 million gallons. The requirements of the City are at present met without raising Loch Katrine or draining from Loch Arklet, and the exercise of these powers is deferred. The water is led from Loch Katrine for 26 miles through tunnels, iron pipes, and aqueducts to the reservoirs at Craig-maddie and Mugdock, which are capable of containing water sufficient to supply the city for 18 and $12\frac{1}{2}$ days respectively. And the total capital expenditure which has attained this result is £3,538,000.

The consumption of water is, of course, enormous, but thanks to excellence of supervision and to the use of good fittings, the domestic consumption has

Water
charges

actually decreased in the last thirty years, and now
stands at somewhat under 40 gallons per head of
population per day. The charge for it is 5d. per £
sterling of rental. On the other hand, the consumption for trade purposes has increased three-
fold in the same time, and as it is charged for at a
rate of 4d. per 1000 gallons, with a minimum
annual charge of £2, the increase in revenue has
tended to relieve the rates. In the year ending
31st May, 1900, the daily average supply of water
was 55,705,063 million gallons ; the gross revenue
was £235,270 13s. 2d. ; the expenditure,
£172,746 5s. 9d. ; and after crediting the sinking
fund a balance of £22,740 9s. 10d. was carried forward to credit of the revenue account. Since 1895
hydraulic pumping works have been maintained in
the central district overlooking Cathedral Square,
which supply water for trade purposes at a pressure
of half a ton to the square inch, with the result of
increasing the power and husbanding the supply.
The excellence of the pressure from the main is
shown by the fact that 600 hoists and 100 hydraulic
presses in the City are worked by it alone.

The benefits of the municipal water supply are
beyond question. The public health of the City
has been enormously improved, and the cheapening
of rates has effected a saving to domestic and trade
consumers which has been calculated at £1,200,000.
The abundance and absolute purity of the water are
benefits which require no figures to prove them.

In the matter of Tramways, the experience of the City has been so far different **Tramways** that while a private Company carried on the tramway undertaking until 30th June, 1894, it did so on a lease from the Corporation. The Company were undoubtedly pioneers, but from 1870, when tramways were first introduced into Glasgow, the Corporation had power to undertake the service for themselves. Under the agreement with the Company the Corporation reserved the right to construct the lines with capital which the Company raised, and the lines have been laid out with skill. Twelve of the main routes enter the triangle at the centre of the City bounded by the three railway stations in Queen Street, St. Enoch's Square, and Gordon Street, and from any one of them each of these routes is reached in a few minutes' walk. The service of cars under the old Company, compared with the present one, was unsatisfactory. The cars were rather small, rather dirty, rather infrequent, and the fares were high. But even so, there was considerable sympathy with the shareholders of the Company when its efforts to obtain a new lease were unsuccessful, and the Corporation decided to undertake the service for themselves. Overtures were made on behalf of the Corporation to take over the Company's plant of cars, horses, etc., but as it was a condition of the offer that the Company should abstain from competing in any way with the Corporation service the sale was not carried through, and the Corporation had to provide them-

[57]

Fares and figures

selves with a gigantic plant within a period of two years, which certainly was not overly long. Still, in that time much can be done, and when the citizens stirred abroad on 1st July, 1894, they found the Corporation service in complete working order. Their New Year's Day delight in hanseling their new property and riding in their coaches and two made the drawings for the day enormous. From the start the service has been a great popular and financial success. The cars are large and clean, the horses in their prime. The hours of drivers and conductors have been reduced to a daily average of ten. The fares have, in many cases, been reduced by half. A halfpenny fare carries one just over half a mile, a penny fare for a mile and three-quarters, while for the maximum fare of threepence one may ride for five miles and a half. In these circumstances the inducement to walk has practically vanished, as the following figures show. On a total mileage of 42½ there ran during the year ending 31st May, 1900, per day of sixteen hours, on the average 316·96 cars and omnibuses. These ran 9,657,429 car miles, carried, against 53,729,472 in the last years of the Company's lease, no less than 127,628,484 passengers (roughly 160 times the population of the City, and about one-fifth of the total number carried on the tramways of England and Wales during 1900), and yielded an average weekly revenue of £8938. At the end of the financial year the balance of revenue over working

expenses was £125,243 19s. 8d., of which **Gas**
£46,568 12s. was placed to general reserve fund.
When the electric system is in complete operation
this handsome result will doubtless be improved,
for the experience of the Tramway Department
has been that the working expenses for electric
haulage are 2·35 pence per car mile less, and the
average return 2·57 pence greater than for horse
haulage. Beyond question, the Corporation have
deserved well of the citizens by their management
of the cars.

In regard to Gas, the Corporation's experience
has been almost identical with that in regard to
water. The first producers were private companies working for dividends and managing their
undertaking so badly that of the gas produced
23·19 per cent. was lost by wastage between the
retort and the consumer. It is not surprising,
therefore, that during the last ten years of their
existence the charge per 1000 cubic feet varied
from 4s. 2d. to 5s. The public outcry was great,
and the Corporation intervened, and after failing to
obtain powers to erect an independent establishment, were authorised to take over the works of
the existing companies, and entered into possession
of them on 1st June, 1869. In the first year the
price was reduced within the City boundaries from
4s. 7d. to 4s. 2d. per 1000 cubic feet, but to consumers outside the boundaries, who were not liable
for the City gas assessment, the charge was 2½d.
more. In the end this additional rate cost the

Gas City in 1891 £202,500 in buying up a rival suburban gas company, founded to serve dissatisfied
consumers, which was a strenuous opponent in that
year of the movement to annex Hillhead and Maryhill to the City.   At present the charge has been
raised from 2s. 2d., at which it had stood for some
years, to 2s. 6d. per 1000 cubic feet, and at this

Temple Gasometers

rate the Corporation now distributes from their
seven works at Dalmarnock, Dawsholm, and
Temple, Tradeston, Pollokshaws, and Old Kil-
patrick some 5400 million cubic feet per day over
an area measuring 16 miles by 10 miles.   The
wastage has been reduced by the use of good fittings
to 9·5 per cent. of the gas produced, and the cost

(in coal) of consumption has been lessened by 36 **Electric** per cent., until it now stands at 11·77 pence per **lighting** 1000 cubic feet. The revenue for the last financial year was £770,002 16s. 10d., which exceeded by £33 the year's expenditure and payment of standing charges.

The supply of gas for illuminating purposes does not, however, exhaust the activities of the Corporation in this field. Since 1885 the department sells or hires gas stoves and fires, with the necessary connections, and has drawn a profit of over £500 annually from this source.

In Electric Lighting, Glasgow, like most British towns, has been distinctly backward. The Corporation only received powers to undertake this business in 1890, and it was not till February, 1895, that the first electric lamps were used for street lighting. Since then considerable progress has been made, and 265 arc lights are in regular use. The power stations number seven, of which the chief is in Wellington Street, and include one recently acquired in the Kelvinside district, where the number of domestic consumers is rapidly increasing. At 31st May, 1900, the total number of consumers was 2852, which showed an increase of 53 per cent. during the year. In the lighting of the streets a great improvement will probably be effected by the electric cars, for presumably where the electric cars go there will the electric light be also. One day the City may look garish at night.

In all great cities the slums, filth, crime, and

City Improve-
ment Trust

disease are in league against the public interest, and when the Corporation was forced by the instinct of self-preservation to establish in 1866 the City Improvement Trust and in 1862 the Health Department it was attacking these allies on both flanks. The private efforts which, prior to 1866, had been made in Glasgow to buy up insanitary areas and lay out new streets, had failed mainly through the lack of the compulsory powers which the Corporation, as the City Improvement Trustees, obtained under their Act of that year. They were empowered to acquire land and raze houses in an area of 88 acres on both sides of the Clyde, containing a population of 51,000 ; to dispose of these lands when cleared ; if need be, to erect new buildings on them, and to dispose of both. Their power of imposing rates was to terminate in 1876, by which time it was expected that their labours would be ended. The demolition of houses, begun in 1870, was prosecuted briskly for three years, and the demand for feus was such that in 1874 it seemed that accounts would be closed with a good balance. But thanks to a crisis in the property market, which made sellers as thick as blackberries, the Trustees found themselves in 1878, when their rating powers had expired, the owners of great unsaleable areas of cleared land, and numbers of the worst tenements in Glasgow. The failure of the City of Glasgow Bank in the following year did not mend the matter, and though an Act in 1880 gave them further borrowing powers and re-

moved the limit on the period of assessment, the City Improve-
Trustees were helpless until 1888, when the ment Trust

— The Foot of the Stockwell

demand for property began to revive.   Meanwhile
their vacant ground had to be nursed at ruinous

City Improve-ment Trust

cost. Finally they were forced to build on it, and here the mischief was that with the high price they had paid for it houses could not be built to pay at rents within the means of the tenants who had been dislodged. But shirking was useless, and small beginnings were made in Drygate and Saltmarket. Now the completed tenements built by the Trustees contain in all 591 houses, of which 185 have one, 367 two, and 39 three rooms, and let respectively at rents averaging £4 10s., £11 14s., and £16 12s. per annum. For single waifs of both sexes Model Lodging-houses have been erected to the number of seven, in which, for a daily charge of 3½d. or 4½d., men have a cubicle to sleep in and the use of kitchen, dining, and recreation rooms, with bath and lavatory accommodation. In the women's lodging-houses the charge is a halfpenny less. In March, 1896, the Trustees widened their sym-pathies by opening a Family Home in St. Andrew Street for widows and widowers with children, providing apartments, which are heated by hot water and lighted by electricity, and undertaking the care of the children during the absence of the parent at work. The revenue from this source increases steadily. The most recent powers of the Trustees have been conferred by an Act of 1897, which authorises them to deal with certain new insanitary areas, and to purchase land near the centre of the City, on which to erect tenements suitable "for the poorest classes." For this pur-pose, seventeen acres have been already acquired.

It remains to add that the Trustees' consistent **Health** **Department** policy has been to refuse to let any of their property as licensed premises.

In public health and decency the operations of the Trust have worked an immense improvement, and the material gain to the City has been quite palpable. Thirty new streets have been made (bearing in many cases the names of illustrious bailies), and twenty-seven have been widened and improved. Alexandra Park, in the East End, on which the Municipal Golf Links are laid out, has been purchased. And the annual cost to the City since 1866 has only been some £24,000.

The other pioneer organisation of the Corporation, the Health Department, was started in 1862. Until that time the City had been visited again and again by hateful epidemics of typhus fever and cholera, and even in that year cholera was in the City. The need for preventive measures was extremely urgent, and the first medical officer of Glasgow, Dr. W. T. Gairdner, now Sir W. T. Gairdner, K.C.B., Emeritus Professor of Medicine in the University, had his hands very full. The beginnings of the organisation were of the smallest. In 1864 Dr. Gairdner's staff numbered an " inspector of nuisances " and three non-medical officers " selected from the police force for special sanitary duty," and his office was two shops rented at £25. At this day the Health Department is housed in the Sanitary Chambers in Montrose Street, and consists of a principal medical officer and assistants, a

F [65]

Fever Hospitals bacteriologist, a veterinary surgeon, and a clerical staff. It manages three hospitals for infectious diseases, where patients are treated at the public expense, with reception and sanitary wash-houses. The medical officer has power to order a tenant to cleanse, purify, and fumigate his dwelling, to remove persons suspected of infectious disease to the Reception Houses in Weaver Street and South York Street, where they are maintained under observation at the City's charges, and to have the household belongings and clothing of suspects treated at the disinfecting stations at Belvidere and Ruchill. Under this latter head an enormous work is performed; some 540,000 articles are disinfected annually, and such was the popular admiration for this form of cleansing that the department were forced to employ " checkers " to prevent the disinfecting stations from being turned into public washing-houses on a grand scale. The actual treatment of disease is undertaken at the four fever hospitals—in Kennedy Street, and at Belvidere (the first Municipal Fever Hospital in Scotland), in the eastern district; at Ruchill (recently completed), in the north-western district; and at Knightswood (acquired by the City in virtue of the Annexation Act of 1891, and under joint management), in the western district. The first two hospitals cost the City annually over £40,000. Ruchill Hospital has been started so recently that accounts of its expenditure are not yet available.

The work of the sanitary inspector and his staff

precedes that of the medical officer. The object of it is by inspection to prevent the occurrence of diseases, and for this reason "nuisances" are hunted down with immense zeal. In short space no one can adequately define this word, but we believe it to include the existence of conditions in buildings or their sanitary arrangements which are inimical to the public health. From the sanitary report for 1899 it appears that what is hidden in the term occurred in the city in 32,437 cases, which shows much diligence on the part of the inspectors. The 25,000 houses which are "ticketed" as having less than the normal amount of cubic air space are constantly inspected ; so, too, are houses in the poor quarters farmed as lodgings ; and factories, workshops, bakehouses, byres, dairies, and milkshops have all their inspectors. The department also prevents, by way of prosecution, the emission of black smoke from manufacturing works, tests drains, vaccinates citizens at public expense, and in a hundred and one ways renders services which are not within the scope of private effort.

Work of Health Department

The disposal of sewage and street refuse, though undertaken by another department, is of a piece with the work of the sanitary authorities. And in this matter the Corporation has been active. Until 1884 the unhappy Clyde was made the tidal cesspool of the city, with consequences unpleasing to the eye and nose. But in 1894 the first sewage purification works were opened at Dalmarnock,

where about one-fifth of the city's sewage, amount-
ing annually to over 4500 million gallons, is
treated, the sludge being converted into manure or
disposed of as unsaleable refuse, while the liquid,
after being converted by chemical and filtering
treatment into a colourless innocuous water (in
which gold fish will live), is run into the Clyde.
Further works, dealing with the area not served at
Dalmarnock, are rapidly approaching completion
on the western side of the city, and within a reasonable time the river will not suffer in smell or
colour from the contributions which Glasgow
makes to its volume. Street refuse is dealt with
at various despatch works of the newest kind.

The work of nearly all the departments whose
activities we have indicated has helped greatly
in improving the City's health. With water pure
and abundant, improved houses (from which
insanitary conditions are carefully removed),
and infectious diseases treated by modern
methods, the death-rate per 1000 inhabitants has,
within the last five-and-thirty years, fallen from
30 or 33 to 21. Glasgow is no longer the happy
hunting-ground of infectious diseases. Cholera
has disappeared, typhus has been practically
exterminated, smallpox, in ordinary years, rarely
occurs, and the death-rate from epidemic
diseases has been reduced by 50 per cent.

In showing, by way of conclusion, how the
services which the Corporation renders are paid,
I may divide them, without much accuracy,

into tangible and intangible services. Under the **Rates**
first head is included the supply of Water, Gas
and Electricity, and of Tramway Cars; under the
second the following groups of incompatibles:—
Police, Sanitary, and Public Health Administra-
tion; care of Roads, Bridges, Parks, Clyde
Embankments, and also of Lunatics; City
Improvement; Prevention of Juvenile Delin-
quency and Diseases of Animals; Registration of
Births, etc., and of Voters; Valuation of Lands;
Prison Payment. The departments which render
the services included under the first head also

Gartnavel Asylum

collect the charges for them. But the method
of charge varies with the service. Thus the
tramway payments are made, as it were, on the
rail. The rate for gas and for water used for
trade purposes depends on the amount consumed,
and, as we have seen, is 2s. 6d. per 1000 cubic feet
for the first, and 4d. per 1000 gallons (with a minimum annual charge of £2) for the second. Water
used for domestic purposes is treated as a
necessity of life, and the charge for it is uniform,
being 5d. per £ of rental for a supply which,
except in dry seasons, is unlimited. Electricity

Rates is also charged for according to amount consumed, on an exaggerated principle of giving a reduction for taking a quantity.

For the intangible services the payment is by rates levied on rental, and collected for the whole city by the Police Department from owners and occupiers. To the latter the rate is 1s. 10½d. per £ on rents under £10, and 2s. 5 13-16d. per £ on rents above that figure. To owners the assessment is 1s. 3 10-32d. In addition to these the householder pays others which are not municipal, viz., Poor rate and School Board rate, and these swell his total of rates to the somewhat formidable figure of 20 per cent. of his rental.

The total sum which the Police Department in 1899-1900 collected as rates was £495,666, and as this was levied on a rental which reached the gigantic figure (already stated) of £4,499,520, it is apparent that the City security for borrowing is extremely good.

It remains to add that the Corporation possesses in the Common Good a source of private wealth which is in no way connected with the ratepayers' purse. "All property and revenues of the Corporation which are not held under special Acts of Parliament nor raised by taxation" come under this head. The capital value, represented by heritable and moveable property, is £1,330,000, of which £360,000 is not ear-marked to special purposes, and the annual revenue is

some £50,000. It is on this source that the **Common Good** Corporation draws when, as in the case of the Tramways or Telephones, it embarks on a new venture.

III

Her Seat of Learning

(1) History

THE University of Glasgow is of honourable **The** antiquity, for in the summer of this year of grace, **founded** 1901, it has celebrated its ninth Jubilee, the first, indeed, which it has troubled itself to remember. And its history is not less honourable than its age.

On the 7th January, 1451, Pope Nicholas V., complying with a request made by his "reverend brother," Bishop Turnbull, of Glasgow, at the instance of his "illustrious and beloved son in Christ, James [Second], King of Scots," set his hand to a Bull ordaining that a University, modelled on that of Bologna, be erected at Glasgow, "a place well suited and adapted to "that purpose, on account of the healthiness of "the climate, the plenty of victuals, and of every- "thing necessary for the use of man." "The reverend brother" and his successors in office were made Rectors and Chancellors, with power and authority over the doctors, masters, scholars,

The
University
founded

and others. The privileges and exemptions enjoyed by the members of Bologna University were extended to those of the new University, and the Bishop was empowered to confer degrees and grant the licence to teach in any University.

Bishop Turnbull made quick use of his power.

Back of the Rottenrow

The University was established, and by the end of 1451 its members, including Chancellor, rector, masters, doctors, and students, numbered more than 80. Indeed, so quickly did they increase that the Crypt of the Cathedral, which the Bishop had allowed them for a meeting-place, within four years could not contain them and was abandoned

[72]

for a house in the Rottenrow which belonged to **The early** the minister of Luss, and until the middle of the **statutes** present century was known as the Old Pedagogy. In 1459 the Faculty of Arts acquired by gift from Lord Hamilton a piece of ground on the east side of the High Street, which, along with other pieces of ground subsequently acquired, was the site of the buildings known now as the Old College. Here, with an interval between 1645-47, when the ravages of the plague in Glasgow drove the entire members of the University to seek asylum first in Irvine, then in Paisley, the University had its home at the heart of the city for nearly three centuries. It was only in 1870 that it stepped westwards to the present buildings on Gilmorehill.

The statutes of the University were first settled in 1482. The students were divided according to their domicile of origin into the four nations of Clydesdale, Teviotdale, Albany, and Rothesay. And these nations elected four procurators to choose a Rector, who, with the nations, elected four deputies to form his Council. The Rectorial Council may be said to have exercised judicial functions, while the Chancellor was the depositary of executive power. There were separate statutes, too, for the individual Faculties; but for nearly two centuries and a half the Faculty of Arts alone had actual existence. The session began in October and ended in July, the students being divided according to their standing into Bejans

[73]

Students and teachers (or "yellow beaks"), Semis, Baccalours, and Magistrands. On passing through the prescribed studies, mainly in logic, morals, and physics, the candidate for a degree was examined by four "Temptatores," of whom two were regents and two were masters, and it was on the faith of their report to the Dean of Faculty that degrees were conferred. The degrees of Licentiate and of Master of Arts were granted at the end of the fourth year, and all who obtained the degree and the licence [to teach] bound themselves to teach in the University for two years; but in time, as the studies grew in importance, some of the masters, termed "Magistri Regentes," remained permanently in residence, and presumably performed the functions of the professors who ultimately succeeded them. The undergraduates lived in the College buildings until these were found too small to contain their numbers, when lodgings were obtained in the town for the superfluous. The letters of lodgings had less competition in those days, for so extortionate were their charges that Bishop Turnbull intervened in the interests of the University, and by means of a committee of Town and Gown fixed a maximum rent.

After the Reformation the University fell on evil times, and despite various benefactions by Queen Mary in 1563, it was, in 1571, still in so desperate a condition that the Town Council conferred upon it certain church lands which they had received from the Queen. At that time its total members amounted to a beggarly fifteen and its rental to £300 Scots (£25 sterling). But better days were at hand. In 1574 Andrew Melville, the first Protestant to hold the office, was appointed Principal, and by his energy and learning succeeded in reviving a decayed institution. At his suggestion Regent Morton secured, in 1577, from King James VI., then in his minority, a "*Nova Erectio*," which made considerable alterations in the constitution, and in large part is still in force. The old grants of land were confirmed. Provision was made for the residence of twelve persons in the College, viz., a Principal (gymnasiarch), three Regents, an economus or steward, four poor students, the Principal's servant, a cook, and a janitor. The Principal was made head of the College, with authority over the Regents and the other members. The Regents were directed to teach distinct subjects, and to abandon the former practice of conducting one batch of students through all the studies. Also, they were forbidden to change their subject annually except at the order of the Principal; and some of their modern successors appear faithfully to have observed the spirit of this injunction in declining to vary the form of their lectures. Provision was further made for the election of the Principal and the Regents, their duties were defined, and their salaries fixed. Similar pro-

[75]

visions were made for the duties and salaries of
the other officials. The steward in particular was
directed to be "rather helpful of the College
interests than his own." This, then, is the Nova
Erectio in bare outline, and to add somewhat to
the picture of the University at that period the
statutes may be cited which provided that
students were to rise at five in the morning, and
to be in bed by a quarter to nine in the evening;
permitted golf, archery, and dramatic representa-
tions, but forbade carding, dicing, billiards, and
bathing, and prescribed Latin as the means of
conversation among the students.

About 1630 the rebuilding of the College was
begun, and funds were raised by subscription from
every kind of person and corporations throughout
the land, from King Charles I. down to the burgh
of Stirling. The King did not, it is true, keep his
promise himself, but Cromwell, while in Glasgow
in 1651, did this for him. Indeed, the Protector
took considerable interest in the University, for
not only did he visit it but he made a grant of
£500 to the building fund. Furthermore, he
heaped coals of fire on the head of the Principal,
Zachary Boyd, who had reviled him in a sermon
preached in the Cathedral on 27th October, 1650,
by inviting him to sup in the evening, and finally
engaging in prayer with him for the space of
three hours, whereby the good Principal was
detained from his bed until three in the following

morning. It is interesting in this connection to note that in 1658 Thurlow, Cromwell's Secretary of State, was elected Chancellor of the University by a majority of the professors, and held office until the Restoration.

The reconstruction of the buildings was completed by 1660, and in the seventeenth century there is little more that deserves mention. In the eighteenth century the University made numerous additions to its professorships, and the faculties, other than that of Arts, began to exchange their state of appearance for one of reality. In the latter half of the century the University was famous in teachers, for Adam Smith, Thomas Reid, the philosopher, and Joseph Black were professors within its gates, while James Watt was "philosophical instrument maker to the University," with a room in the tower.

In the nineteenth century the University, changed in equipment, habitation, and constitution, has seen her fame grow. Her chairs have been increased by eighteen new foundations, one of them unique in Britain, a chair of Naval Architecture. Her ancient quarters in the High Street were abandoned in 1870 for the buildings on Gilmorehill, to which additions are now planned to provide laboratories for medical and scientific teaching. And, in common with the other Scottish Universities, she has been purged of many mediæval survivals by the Universities Commission, which regulated afresh the gradua-

[77]

The University sity in more recent times
tion in all her faculties, provided for the foundation of new chairs, reformed the method and scale of her professors' remuneration, and enabled her to

High Street

make Queen Margaret's College for women a part of herself, and to admit its students to her degrees.

[78]

In her teachers she has been fortunate, for since the days of Adam Smith and Thomas Reid she has numbered among her Arts professors the Humanists, Sir Daniel Sandford, Edmund Lushington, and Sir R. C. Jebb; the great exponent of Idealism, Edward Caird; and Lord Kelvin, the greatest physicist of his time, and for fifty years her most famous teacher. In the Medical faculty, the tradition connected with William Cullen and Joseph Black in last century has been carried on in this by Allen Thomson, Lord Lister, Sir W. T. Gairdner, and, in the faculty of Divinity, John Caird, afterwards her Principal, was a pearl in her crown. At the beginning of the new century her hopes are bright. Her students number nearly 1700 men and 350 women. She has thirty-two professors and forty-one assistants, and if the West of Scotland maintains its traditional name for generosity, her credit-balance, which in 1899-1900 was £138, will be changed into something less depressing.

The Scottish Universities are nothing if not national democratic institutions. Their students are drawn from every class in the community. Each man is as good as his neighbour, and, except in the matter of studies, is left by the University authorities to his own devices. He may live where he pleases—at home, in lodgings, at an hotel, at a settlement. No one inquires, for no one cares. Nor is there a standard of good form which prescribes to him his manners, his accent,

The Scots
Universities

or his dress. In these affairs the individual is the
sole, and often incompetent, judge. But, on the
other hand, the *esprit de corps* which comes from
living, as it were, in family is not conspicuous.
The University is rather regarded as an avenue to
a degree, and it is sometimes forgotten that the
student has duties towards her beside punctual
payment of fees and close attendance at classes.
But no sooner is this said than one must recant
and distinguish. There are universities and
universities, and those which are situated in great
manufacturing or commercial towns are different
from the others. Thus St. Andrews and Edinburgh
(perhaps even Aberdeen) would resent this
description of their students, in some respects
with justice. St. Andrews is a small town com-
posed chiefly of University and Links, elements
alike fruitful of conflict and rivalry. The University is also small, and though the students do live
out of College, nearly every man knows the other
and generally has him for neighbour. And so
there is an excellent spirit of good-fellowship and
pride in the University, such as is found in
Southern schools of learning. Edinburgh,
certainly, is a large town, but its main industry,
as a shrewd Lord Provost said, is education, and
the University therefore occupies in it a place of
great and natural distinction. Among the
students, too, there is a large foreign—in the
sense of English and Colonial—element, and the

native individualism of its Scots student may be yielding to the new influences which that element exerts. Of Aberdeen it is hard to judge; but it has produced a College poet whose verses represent the University life as existing and attractive, and we are glad to take his word for it. Remains Glasgow, of which, we think, what we have written above is true. Indeed, it is difficult to see how it could be otherwise. Founded when the town was a handful of houses set about the Cathedral, the University has seen the town grow into an enormous city, with interests alien from hers. Unlike the University Colleges, say, of Manchester and Liverpool, she is in no particular, except perhaps that of buildings, the product of the city's greatness. And hence it is small wonder if the ordinary Glasgow man regards her as less important than his docks, his river, or his ship-building yards. And what the ordinary man thinks of her, the student, his son, is apt to think also. But both are wrong, for neither has imagination. If the City did not make the University, it was she who helped to make the City. For she set a standard of education for the whole West of Scotland throughout the century, and the intelligence which she fostered, if she did not actually train, exploited the resources of Lanarkshire and made Glasgow. It is this task of setting a standard in education which she performs still with admirable success. She does not

G

The Univer-
sity and the
City profess to give the highest training in the Arts
faculties, or to fit her students for the solely
intellectual life, nor does she turn them into
leaders of research. And for the obvious reason
that, though she may lead in the intellectual, she
cannot create callings in the practical life. What
she does profess and what she achieves is to give
to all her students in the Arts faculty a general
education, and to those who take her Honours
degree a culture which in most of the subjects is
very far from low, and in philosophy is very near
the summit. Her misfortune is that she cannot
afford to gather round her a body of young men
devoting themselves to the "breadless" studies,
whose exertions would tend to raise both the
effectiveness of her teaching and the value of her
degrees. But who knows what may happen when
the millionaire, who is also philosopher, comes to
die!

And as our survey is now complete,
we may form a judgment of the place
which the University occupies in Scotland
to-day, of the function which she performs in
the system of national education. In the faculties which provide a professional training her
reputation in Scotland is high. It is true that in
England and abroad, Edinburgh, thanks to her
famous past and to her extra-mural school competing with the University, is recognised as the
leading medical school in the kingdom; but in

1900-1901 only forty-four per cent. of her students were Scots. Glasgow, on the other hand, has only a slight proportion of foreigners. In science, pure and applied, Lord Kelvin has made Glasgow's reputation, and for years has attracted students from America and Japan. In law, her teaching staff, though absurdly small, has succeeded in maintaining the standard of her teaching and of her degree as high as that in Edinburgh, where a staff at least twice as large dwells in the shadow of the Supreme Court. In the Divinity faculty she has a tradition for Liberal Theology which she owes to the teaching, in that faculty and out of it, of John and Edward Caird. We may conclude this survey by saying quite judicially, that the University is in sound health, and that with her new equipment of laboratories she need fear no rival north or south of Tweed.

The University in 1901

(2) The Student

If you turn from the University to the student, you will find him, in the main, young, quiet-living, industrious, earnest, and immature. These qualities sometimes desert him in part when he is one of a crowd, as incompetent teachers know. Is there not the story, well authenticated, of the conscientious assistant who read his professor's lecture without skipping a word, while the class paid attention by singing two-and-thirty choruses

The undergraduate

[83]

within the hour? But professors who are competent command instant respect. And of them, as
a body, the ordinary student stands in awe. He
rarely meets them in a capacity other than formal,
and if his attitude in personal intercourse is rather
that of a schoolboy to his master, you can hardly
wonder. With classes of 150 men, it makes little
difference whether you invite them to your house
in droves of twenty or not at all. They remain so
many strangers with different names in your class
roll. Further, the student's feeling that his professor differs from him in social position, keeps
him shy and gauche, and just a little suspicious.
Yet when his love is won, it is given for ever, and
some professors would blush if they could hear
their men speak of them.

His life is plain and hard, and rather poor in
colour. His class at eight a.m. calls him early
from his bed—how early, he who comes to it by
train from the suburbs will tell you. And what,
after all, comes he out for to see? The tardy
moon lighting him up the College hill, the windy
quadrangle all dark, the lighted class-room
windows, a brisk janitor selling the College
Magazine, the College bell, clattering for five short
minutes after the hour has struck, its sudden stop,
the scramble of men to enter while yet there is
time, the roll-call, the lecture, the bent heads of
the note-takers, the scraping of their anxious feet
lest a word be missed, the rustling of a sporting
paper, the smell of wet waterproof in the hot air,

the intolerable dreichness of (let us say) the Con- **College**
veyancing Statutes, and then—happy release!— **relaxations**
the College clock booming out the hour, and once
more the rain and the wind in the quadrangle.
No handsome reward this for early rising!
Classes meet all day long from 8 a.m. till 5.30 p.m.,
and if our friend has a spare hour, and is eager for
work, he goes across to the gaunt, warm Reading-
room, where a comrade with a " call " may invite
him to defend everlasting as against eternal
punishment, or another, with a foible for jokes,
may, in absent-mindedness, tell him the same new
story thrice in sixty minutes. Or, if he is content
with relaxation, he may go over to the Union
where, for five shillings per annum, he will find
many comforts which his landlady denies him.
Here from noon onwards he may play billiards, a
game under suspicion with the authorities, who
forbade it in the mornings less classes might be
depleted. Here he may eat meals as cheap as his
landlady's, and less nasty. Here, too, o' Friday
nights, in the Debating Hall, he may learn to
know his own voice, and express his views on the
Gothenburg System, the Uses of Protoplasm, or
the Economics of One Man One Job; or, again, as
member for the Rotten Boroughs, defend or
denounce the policy of His Majesty's Ministers.

But these things are pursued, not as ends in
themselves, but as relaxations. For the fear of
examinations encompasses the student behind and
before, and paints his life drab. While it is yet

[85]

The Rectorial Election day he worketh, and still more when the night cometh. For his admission to a Degree Examination depends, not on payment of fees only, but on a fair attendance at classes and honest, if undistinguished, performance of the work prescribed in them. The authorities are stricter now, and even a Stevenson could hardly cajole a " ticket " out of the humanest professor.

Yet once in three years the winter session almost opens with a Rectorial Election, and exam-ridden students are changed into primitive men leading a joyous existence. The Lord Rector is the highest official in the University under the Chancellor, the candidates almost invariably politicians of eminence unconnected with the University, and put forward by the College political clubs. The electors are the matriculated students, male and female, divided, according to birthplace, into the ancient nations of Glottiana, Rothseiana, Transforthiana, and Loudoniana. The election is unique in Great Britain. The voting is open, and bribery and corruption are not even technically prohibited. The clubs seldom lack funds, for the party organisations in the West of Scotland shrewdly see that their subscriptions are investments. The campaign is actual warfare, involving scrimmages, pease-meal battles, storming and wrecking of alternate committee rooms, and heroic defences with water hoses and fists. Nor is invective disdained, and play-bills on prominent walls, shedding new light on the character of the

University Gate, Dublin

notable students, afford the unpugnacious some **The poll**
quiet entertainment. The polling day takes one
straight to Alice in Wonderland. The young
elector need not, and does not, walk to the
University. His jacket turned inside out, a red
or blue cap on his head, he buys a supply of
pease-meal in convenient bags, and drives at his
club's expense in hansom, four-wheeler, omnibus,
or char-a-banc at his pleasure. His route is traced
in flour. For want of opponents, umbrellas covering quiet people are fair, but hardly sporting, game.
At the College gates, however, his own turn comes,
and he has luck if, in that pandemonium, he is not
made a dusty miller and his driver retains his hat.
Even if he is a girl, he is not spared, and to girls
of mettle this is a great delight. At the polling
station he may find his party in force, and, by a
phalanx, holding the door against their opponents.
His way to his vote may then lie literally over the
heads of his own men. Once within the room, a
grave professor informs him of the choice of
candidates, and records his fancy for him. Noon
closes the poll, and when the votes are counted,
the Principal, from the balcony over the main doorway, announces, in a passionless voice, that the
Right Hon. The Earl of Thistle and Garter is
elected Lord Rector of the University by a
majority in three nations. The cheering may be
heard in Govan, and the defeated leaders walk
down the hill, grave, silent Stoics impervious to
jibe. Yet by nightfall they so far command their

The poll

faces as to assist with outward-seeming gaiety in leading the torchlight procession which moves from the College with song and smoke and flame, storms a Panorama or music-hall, and perchance ends in jail.

By the next week the examination fog is again over the University, and the primitive man, turned student, is again at his labours.

IV

The Clyde

(1) The Making of the River

"Glasgow made the Clyde"

IN face of our admirable tag, the unction of Clyde Trust oratory, and the insistence of guide-books, one ventures with timidity on the point that the Clyde existed before its epigram, and even had, perhaps, a certain use in the world before Glasgow decided to "make it."   Like the sister rivers, Tweed and Annan, which rise from the heart of the same bare field in the Moffat highlands, the Clyde was a pleasant salmon stream that tumbled down the hills much as it does to-day, but broad and shallow as it neared the sea, and fordable a good twelve miles below Glasgow Bridge at the ancient castle of Dunglass. To-day it is a deep and brown river that runs past the old ruin, bearing from the building yards in its upper reaches the world's greatest liners and battleships, which pass to the

[88]

sea with never a dip of their flags to the slender **The conquest** monument rising from the castle ivy in honour of **of the river** Henry Bell, the father of them all.

In the old days the Clyde did by Glasgow as well as it could ; on the whole a good deal. It provided drinking water, granted a livelihood to a colony of fishers, and bore the flat wherries, with occasional pauses on the shoals, to and from the ships, which ended their voyages some fifteen miles short of the City. When the elders of the kirk inculcated valuable moral lessons by "dowking" an erring sister over the brig-end it soused her righteously. It had a way, too, at times, of actively reminding the burghers of its existence, for even in 1782 it drove the dwellers in Saltmarket and Gorbals to take to boats out of their topmost windows. But in 1816 it rose in flood for the last time. The plans for its conquest were maturing, and men already at work dredging its channel. From that time the Clyde has played the servant. A little spate, a little ice, and once a Clutha landing-stage sent to its account—these are the mild variants on its dumb, steadfast, uniform obedience. It bears the great steel ships on its narrow waters to the heart of a "sea-born" city that was born 20 miles from salt water. In Tweed and Annan the salmon may leap and children paddle with clean feet—the Clyde is a tide in the affairs of men.

The transformation that has happened to the river, though somewhat longer in the working, is little less wonderful (when one considers it) than

"The little key at the Broomielaw"
many of those told by Scheherazadè to the Sultan Schahriar. A century and a half ago Glasgow seemed as unlikely to become a seaport as Stirling or Dumfries. A hundred years since there was a depth of fourteen inches in the harbour. Only the other day died an old Clyde pilot who, as a lad, had waded across the river where he now steered vessels whose draught was five times his stature.

We will take up the story of the Clyde's "making" at 1662, a convenient date, for then the Council determined, "for many guid reasons and considerations, for the more commodious laidining and landing of boats, that there be ane little key builded at the Broomielaw"; and this was done at a cost of £166 13s. 4d. The event was also of significance in another light, as it was advised by the said Council that the Dean of Guild, in completing the same, should "try for oakin timber aither in the Hie Kirk or back gallerie." One feels in the very words of the resolution that the far-seeing magistrates had already parted company with the older ideal, and the prosperity of the City was no longer to be dependent on the preaching of the Word.

Prior to this time Glasgow had not troubled herself much with ships and shipping. But she was not wholly heedless of their necessities. Thus in 1566 detachments of the inhabitants of Glasgow, Renfrew, and Dumbarton had laboured to open up a formidable sandbank at Dumbuck, living during their operations in huts by the river-side. But in the reign of the British Solomon, and at the time **Wanted, a port** when the early Scots emigrant was making out for his fair share in the plantation of Ulster, an important step was taken. For it is recorded that the magistrates, hearing that James Inglis, the Provost, was to ride to Cowross, desired him to bring one Henrie Crawford to the town at the town's expense, to " sie and consider the river, how the same may be helpit." Again there was a valiant attempt on the ford of Dumbuck, but that obstruction was to tax the wit of the citizens and throttle the navigation of the river till the eighteenth century was sped. " Irne, hogheidis, and other necessaries " were provided, and tried in vain. In 1656 Tucker, as we have seen, found that the shallowness of the river, " mineasing and filling up every day," was very harmful to the City's commerce. Vessels could not come nearer than fourteen miles, and must discharge their cargoes into flat-bottomed boats, which took them to Glasgow. Indeed, for a time Irvine, on the Ayrshire coast, was the outport of Glasgow, but in 1660 the expense and delay of land carriage between the towns showed our City Fathers that by hook or crook a nearer port must be found or made. Accordingly they made overtures in that year to Dumbarton, but the Council of the burgh refused to entertain their proposals, on the prudent ground that the influx of mariners would raise the price of provisions to the inhabitants. Eight years later

The awakening the alternative course was taken. In the neighbourhood of Greenock thirteen acres of land were purchased, a harbour built, the first Scots graving-dock constructed, and the whole to this day bears the name of Port-Glasgow. After building their "little key," the Council began to take the river shipping more seriously, and in 1667 went the length of ordering a register to be kept "of each ship that came in this river of Clyde."

In the century which followed, the tobacco trade rose, flourished, and fell, and the City made a beginning in industries. Her ships began their ventures across the Western Ocean to the Americas, round the Cape to the Far East, and continued to ply across more native waters to the Continent. And the wings of her trade brought Glasgow to undreamed-of havens of prosperity. Yet all the while the Clyde had been left to fend for herself. The lower river had not been uncared for. The channel between Port-Glasgow and Garvel Point had been "bowied and perched," and the island of Little Cumbrae had been given a lighthouse. But, as before, cargoes still came to Glasgow from the lower river in lighters, which floated up and down in a tide or two. The old enemy, the shoal at Dumbuck, had not been removed in spite of all efforts to "wede" it.

In 1755 Glasgow at last awoke to the importance of her river, and that year of grace saw the new order beginning, for Smeaton, the eminent engineer, was employed to report on its state. His account gives us some idea of what the Council of these times had to face. Of the twelve different shoals between Glasgow and Renfrew, the two worst were at Pointhouse Ford—now the launching-ground of ten thousand ton vessels—where the water was fifteen inches at low tide, and at another part of the harbour, where the minimum depth was eighteen inches. Smeaton straightway advised canal methods, and planned a lock to be placed four miles below the town. Parliament was petitioned for powers " to construct locks and dams, cleanse, scour, and straighten, enlarge, and improve the river from Dumbuck Ford to the Bridge of Glasgow "; and this, the first Act dealing with Clyde navigation, was passed in 1759. The Act, however, was of little value to our Council, as the powers it gave to levy dues were dependent on the locking of the Clyde, and Smeaton's scheme fell before the strong opposition offered by Glasgow herself and the lower Clyde burghs, the father of James Watt being one of the strongest objectors. It is curious to note how the canal idea continued to occur in the history of the river improvement. In 1836 it would seem that Glasgow was to forerun Manchester in the matter of ship canals, as a most elaborate scheme was propounded to cut a deep waterway from Bowling Bay, on the north bank, to run parallel with the Clyde and enter the docks at Broomielaw; but again the plans came to naught, chiefly through a wholesome distrust of the behaviour of the steamboats of the time.

Canal proposed

[93]

John Golborne
of Chester

To return to our narrative. After Smeaton
had made his proposals, nothing was done until
in 1768 arrived one John Golborne of Chester.
To him Glasgow owes much, and when all
honest men get their due he shall have his monument. He was the pioneer of the navigable Clyde,
and laid down the policy which was to influence all
future operations. He discouraged the canal
system altogether. " I shall proceed," he writes,
" on these principles of assisting nature when she
cannot do her own work, by removing stones and
hard gravel from the bottom of the river where it
is shallow, and contracting the channel where it is
worn too wide. . . . By these means, easy and
simple in themselves, and without laying a re-
straint on nature, I humbly conceive that the river
Clyde may be deepened so as to have four feet, or
perhaps five feet, up to the Bridge at low water."
His system of contracting the river was by the
construction of a large number of rubble jetties,
in the belief that the intermediate spaces would
be filled up with sand carried down by spates and
silt brought up by the tides. The gravel shoals
were to be loosened or removed by dredging. As
the first Act made the drawing of rates contingent
on the construction of Smeaton's lock and dam
being completed, the Council, before proceeding
with Golborne's scheme, were compelled to apply
for further powers and licence to deepen the river
to the extent of seven feet.

In 1773 Golborne was again called in and, for

the sum of £2300, contracted to remove Dum- **Golborne's**
buck Ford, and leave a depth of six feet of water **operations**
in its place. He blocked up the south passage at
Dumbuck, and after the bottom soil had been
loosened by dredging, the increased current soon
ground down a deep channel on the north. His
operations were crowned with success, for in
1781, when planning a further scheme, he made
soundings, and found to his great satisfaction
fourteen feet of water on the old ford. He also
discovered that the spaces between many of the
jetties were grass-grown—which reclaimed land
was afterwards to cost the Clyde Trust a bonnie
penny when they had to purchase the old avelus
from the riparian proprietors during widening
operations. Golborne's estimate for the entire
operations was roughly £11,400, a heavy
sum at the time, which the Council seem
to have disbursed with proper enterprise.
He himself received the sum of £240 for
his advice and reports, and the Council awarded
him an additional £1500 for deepening the river
ten inches more than he was bound to do by contract. He was also presented with a silver cup,
and his son had £100 for his services. The old
engineer, one is glad to note, seemed very satisfied
with his treatment by the Council. "It made a
lasting impression on my mind," he writes, in the
business phraseology of his century, "and I hope
that the small tribute of my endeavour to promote
the trade and navigation of the opulent City of

Glasgow will be accepted as the overflowing of a grateful heart." Lest we be too much puffed up with pride over the making of this river of ours, let it be remembered that John Golborne was an Englishman.

Looking back over the records of river improvement in the nineteenth century, and the multitude of counsellors who sometimes brought anything but wisdom to their task, one is moved to admiration for the Council's bold initiative in adopting, at a time when no vessel of burden came up to the Broomielaw, and the revenue from the river was less than £10 per annum, a scheme of improvement which should cost, by first estimate, no less than £8640. Quite as admirable was the Council's conduct of the operations when once they had been sanctioned and commenced. Golborne had their confidence, and, unlike most engineers who worked at that day for municipal authorities, he was left to execute his plans in his own way, with not so much as a superior bailie to interfere with, or dictate to, him.

After Golborne came Rennie, who further contracted the river by connecting the ends of the jetties with a dyke running parallel to the banks. Telford and Reddie followed, and in 1824 a second Englishman was consulted, who gave the weight of his counsel to undo all the good that Golborne and his successors had done. He advised the breaking up of the dykes and allowing the tide to flow into its ancient recesses, but feared that the

Clyde was ruined, and he, J. Whidbey, had been called in too late. Enter the Clyde Trust

In 1840 the management of river affairs passed from the Town Council to a separate board of guardians called the Clyde Navigation Trust, who also claim our admiration for their excellent scent for fallacies. After Whidbey's plan was dismissed, the ship canal and sundry other schemes were mooted, but wisdom abode with the Trustees, and these also were put aside. Then they had to fight for their own hand against the representatives of the Lord Commissioners of the Admiralty, who arrived on the Clyde in 1846 with drastic ideas of improvement—one of which was to make a drawbridge for the passage of steamers through Glasgow Bridge; and also against one Captain Washington, Examining Commissioner, who came with a view of eliciting facts to support the scheme of establishing in London a Central Board for the control of the whole harbours of Britain. "These gentlemen from a distance," as the Trustees dubbed them in a heated rejoinder to the official report, were successfully withstood, and sent home with a good Scots flea in their lug.

Meantime great events were moving on this narrow strip of water. Henry Bell's "Comet" had set the Clyde on fire—and it has been smoking ever since. To keep pace with the development of steam navigation all the energies of the city were directed towards the one problem,

H

Dredging the deepening of the river, and practically all
the improvements in the first half of the nineteenth century meant nothing more. Once the
depth of sixteen feet had been attained, and
Glasgow had consequently become a port open
to all shipping, the Trust's attention was turned
to providing dock accommodation. But though
the opening of great tidal docks has seemed the
chief development in the past forty years, dredging has gone on steadily all the time. In their
recent schemes the Trust has recognised
that the two matters act automatically, and that
every foot added to the depth of the fairway
demands an equivalent in dock space. At the
beginning horses and ploughs were called
into use for dredging when the banks were
bare at low water—perhaps the only profitable
form of " ploughing the sands " that has been
recorded ;   then   the   " porcupine " plough,
worked by hand capstans from the river-side ; and
later, when Glasgow owned a tug of her own, a
harrow was attached to the stern by tackle, the tug
" setting off by the tide, tearing up the bottom as
far as requisite."   Then the boat steamed back
and started again. In 1824 the first steam dredger
began its work, dredging to a depth of 10 feet 6
inches. Nowadays a depth of 30 feet can be easily
reached.

The formation of docks in the harbour of Glasgow had been recommended by every engineer of
standing for sixty years, yet it was only in 1867

GLASGOW OF FACT

Docks that there was opened the first dock—a small tidal basin covering about five acres on the south side of the river. Ten years later a larger undertaking was completed, and the Queen's Dock at Stobcross took in its first vessel. The prosperity of the river revenues is indicated by the fact that nearly a million and a half was spent in constructing these docks. The trade of the port increased so swiftly that in a few years it was found necessary to add another and larger set of tidal basins to the harbour accommodation. These were dug on the south side, and opened by the Duke of York in 1897, and hence bear the name of the Prince's Dock. "All the modern conveniences" to shippers are provided here, and when Harbour Board deputations visit the Clyde it is here that the purple patches in the after-dinner speeches are dyed. The total water area of Prince's Dock, it may be added, is about 35 acres, and the length of quayage 2·13 miles. The stigma that vessels damaged in Glasgow required to go to Greenock for repair in public graving-dock was removed in 1875, when the Trust opened their first one in Govan ; the second was completed in 1886 ; and the third, which has a length of 880 feet, and has accommodated the "Saxonia," a 14,000-ton Cunarder, was opened a few years later.

In addition to the quay fronting the river, the Trust thus owns and maintains three graving-docks and a patent slip, and three tidal docks— Kingston, Queen's, and Prince's—all of which can

be entered at any state of the tide.   The total Work of the
water area in the basins is 185 acres, and the quay- Trust
age is over seven miles.   There is a minimum
depth of 20 feet at low water in the channel
between Port-Glasgow and the lower harbour, and as there is a tidal range of 11 feet,
vessels drawing as much as 27 feet are able (with
a fair measure of luck) to pass in safety.
An important result of the work on the
river is that the time of high water, which
in 1800 was three hours behind Port-Glasgow,
is now only one hour later.   To maintain a uniform depth from Glasgow Bridge to
the western limit of their jurisdiction at Cardross
Burn, the Trust's dredging plant is most modern
and extensive.   Ten dredgers are constantly at
work, and the sludge which they raise is loaded
into two-and-twenty hopper barges, and by them
deposited in the open sea off Garroch Head, in
Cumbrae, some fifty miles from the City.   The
cost of dredging operations is the heaviest item in
the Trust's expenditure.   Last year's maintenance
account was £41,957.   The Trust also maintains
a fleet of small twin-screw passenger steamers
called " Cluthas," after the Gaelic name for Clyde,
which carry passengers from Victoria Bridge to
Whiteinch, a distance of $3\frac{1}{2}$ miles, for one penny.
The cross-river traffic is served by numerous small
ferries, and by two vehicular ferries with elevating
decks (of which one has drawn from a local rhymer
the apostrophe, " the noble Finnieson, the Hero of

Finance the Clyde "). Among the odds and ends of the
Trust's inventory the curious will find one small
yacht for the use of distinguished visitors, two
diving-bells, one floating digger, and one paddle
tug, which, although in its fiftieth year, can still
turn in its own length with the best of them.

It is not, of course, with its own money that the
Trust has constructed its works, for, like that of
every other modern undertaking, its business is
conducted by means of borrowed capital, and some
idea of the magnitude of its enterprises may be
formed when we say that in the current year it
pays interest on no less than £5,790,187, while its
borrowing powers amount to £7,250,000. The
capital expenditure on river improvement and
works from 1810 to 1900 has been £7,430,702.
Of this amount, £2,937,271 has been spent in the
construction of docks and quays, £1,656,080 on
dredging plant and dredging, £1,535,253 on purchase of ground, while it has cost Glasgow £89,153
to obtain powers from Westminster to carry
through her plans, deepen the river, and so let
Glasgow flourish—in short, to mind her own business. The Trust's revenues have swollen vastly
from year to year. In 1870 the annual income was
£164,093; in 1880, £223,709; and at the close of
the last financial year no less than £441,419—an
amount which touched high-water mark of the
Trust's prosperity, and left a profit of £42,236 on
the year's working. Tonnage dues on vessels contributed £95,606, and on goods £234,931. The

harbour passenger steamers brought in £12,002, the cost of maintenance being £10,662. Ferries have never been a very paying arm of the Trust's service, and it appears at present as though it would like to be relieved of them by the Corporation for the free transit of the lieges, the plausible argument being that the citizen at Finnieston has as much right to cross the river free as he who dwells by the bridges. Last year the ferries yielded £15,045, while the expenditure amounted to £14,706. The graving-dock brought in £19,764 at a cost of £4300; and the cranes £15,509, with £10,236 expenditure. Altogether, the finances of the Trust are very sound, the rates it levies moderate to all comers and a " bargain " to liners; and if enterprises further down the river have reared white elephants to their sorrow, the Trust has had no traffic with these peculiarly expensive monsters.

It is difficult to estimate Glasgow's position among British ports. If you take the matter of vessels on her registry she comes third, Liverpool and London being her only superiors. In 1899, the last returns available, 1172 vessels, aggregating 1,135,443 tons, owned Glasgow as port of registry. As regards the amount of tonnage entered and cleared, foreign, colonial, and coastwise, Glasgow has four superiors in the Navigation Returns— London, Liverpool, Cardiff, and the Tyne ports. Her figures are—cleared, 11,078 vessels, aggregating 3,884,708 tons; entered, 10,876 vessels,

The Renfrew
Bill

aggregating 3,550,146 tons. The contributions of
her shipbuilding yards to the world's tonnage
we deal with elsewhere.

In recent years the Trust has known the bitter
taste of the sea of trouble. The accommodation
of its docks was denounced as insufficient, and the
royal burgh of Renfrew, which the Trust had
hitherto known only as the recipient of an annual
payment of £214 3s. of good Clyde Trust money
in name of compensation for "fishings" damaged
in the early 'fifties, applied to Parliament for
powers to construct a dock in its own neighbourhood which should make good the deficiencies of
Glasgow. The Trust succeeded in its opposition
to the Bill, and by reaction was itself stung into
energy. It promoted a Bill to construct a dock at
Shieldhall, on the south side close to the City, and
at Clydebank on the north side, and, to its sur-
prise, found the unsubdued burgh again opposing
it with its former scheme. The fight issued with
some success to both applicants. The Renfrew
and Clydebank schemes were sanctioned, while
that for Shieldhall was refused. In the present
year the approval of Parliament is sought for an
agreement between the Trust and the promoters of
the Renfrew Dock, which allows the former, in
return for defraying the promoters' expenses and
admitting two representatives of the burgh of Renfrew to membership of the Trust, to take over the
Renfrew Harbour undertaking. In this way the
Trust's virtual monopoly of the docks on the Clyde,

which, as creator of the river, it clearly deserves, will be maintained intact.

The constitution of the Trust has been another cause of complaint, which, however, is in a fair way to be removed. The position is this: Although in 1840 the control of the harbours and river passed from the Town Council to the newly formed Clyde Trust, the City remained the ruling power in the deliberations of that body, for of the

33 members 24 were elected by the Town Council. Eighteen years later, when the Trust obtained a Consolidation Act from Parliament, a strong appeal for representation was made by the shipowners and harbour ratepayers in the City, and in the result the constitution of the Trust was altered to its present form. The number of its members was reduced from 33 to 25, of whom 10 are elected by the Town Council, 9 by the ratepayers, and 2 each by the Chamber of Commerce, Merchants' House,

and Trades' House. The Town Council is thus still
strongly represented. The Lord Provost is *ex
officio* the chairman, and a seat on the Trust, which
is regarded as the Upper House in the City's affairs,
is esteemed a precious thing by the members of
the Council, and the best men in that body are
always eager for election. But the old agitation
for an increased representation of shipowners
and payers of harbour rates has of late been revived,
and the Trust has so far yielded to this as to apply
in its present Bill to Parliament for power to
amend its constitution. It is proposed to increase
the number of members by 8, of whom 6 shall be
elected by the shipowners and ratepayers of the
City, and, as we have seen, 2 by the burgh of
Renfrew. The Trust will then, as in 1840, consist
of 33 members. It is not impossible that the Town
Council will object to this amendment, which would
still further reduce the voting power of its representatives, and over the head of it there may be a
struggle in Parliament between the bodies which,
as an honoured Trustee has put it, have been
" hand-maidens one with another in the conduct
of that great progress, commercial and otherwise,
that this district has exhibited during the last half-
century." Hand-maidens, of course, should not
fight, except in defence of their mistress, and we
believe these shrewd spinsters will recognise
this; indeed, we are confident that they will
compose their difference, remembering that com-
promise is the silver lining of every business cloud.

(2) The Harbour

Having glanced conscientiously at the develop- **Pictorial**
ment of that far-seeing idea, the canalisation of
the Clyde, let us set down some impression
of what it has made the harbour of to-day.

We must out with it at the beginning, that
Glasgow has neither the most picturesque nor
most beautiful harbour in the world. Nature had
not been kind to it in providing even the bare
necessities of the business, and when man took
the matter in hand the aesthetic side was

Suspension Bridge

furthest from his calculations. Its only asset
of beauty is the number and variety of the hills
which rise on either side, and the modern view
from the river of the great city spreading itself
to the sun on every slope would, no doubt—if the
smoke were away, the sheds down, and foreground
tenements levelled—be most imposing. But,
as matters stand, that, too, is lost to us, so he who
would spend a profitable day in the harbour must
either be one whose tastes are inquiring and practical, or, on the other hand, a modern romanticist

Royalty in the Clyde of what—with a bow to Mr. Kipling—we may call " the nine-fifteen " school. It is a place of short perspectives, of drooping smoke wreathes, long lines of sheds crowded by blank tenements, docks that are never free from a sediment of coal dust, of shipbuilding yards, sheer-legs and steam cranes, patent slips and engine shops. And the river, tamed and governed, and almost as dead slow as the legend of the notice boards on its banks ordains ; a dingy, wavering space where ships are seen out of all right proportion, where liners roar in exasperation at dredgers, and Cluthas squeak at ferries, where pilots' hair turns grey ; and whence, if your summer be dry, arises that which makes a man from Manchester feel at home, but only him. In winter, on the foggy days, when lamps set in the shed roofs are hid from the ground, and ships grope in the reaches, it is a cavern filled with wailing and strange cries. Literature has done nothing for the harbour ; nor, if you except two immemorial occasions when a Sovereign of the country arrived at the City by river, has history gilded its waters with a single memory. Those royal visits are somewhat widely separated, the first being that of King Alexander with his fleet, which, according to Fordoun, brought up at Glasgow in safety when on a punitive expedition to the wilds of Argyllshire ; and the other that of Queen Victoria, who, in passage to Balmoral, sailed up to the West Street quay in a craft which, to modern eyes, looks in the print almost as old-fashioned as King Alexander's. Beyond these, **Govan water-side** however, the only pageant the harbour knows is that of a Sunday school trip or a Harbour Board deputation. Its past is one of Highland wherries and single oscillating engines.

There is but one picturesque touch in the place. At the point where a dingy board informs the master or mate (holding a Pilotage Certificate within the meaning of the Act) in command of an incoming steamer that he is now amenable to the harbour bye-laws, a little row of crow-stepped, whitewashed cottages, the last remnant of the old salmon-fishing village of Govan, is seen high and dry above the ferry conduit. Time was when the Clyde water ran by their doors, and the ferryman who lived here pushed his way between a fleet of fishers' cobbles. Hither the Glasgow citizen journeyed through fields to make a day of it on holidays--and a night of it, too, for the ale of one John M'Nair, of Govan, had a wide repute in its time. Now these houses stand in the heart of the shipbuildingest burgh in the world, and the whole population of the old village could be tucked away in any of the liners that come and go with every tide.

But once past Govan you have no further pointer to sentiment ; you are on the threshold of something very different from the quaint or the picturesque. This highway to the city is avenued by works in throes and turmoil. Chaotic masses of ship frames, pyramids of timber, jibs of cranes,

The work-a-day river

vast engine shops, legions of masts and chimneys shrouded in a greyness under what some one has called the engineering skies of Glasgow; and this greyness rotates and clangs with the whirring of machinery and the pounding of hammers. The water is a dull, oily bronze, sluggishly moving between the walls of the quays, washing in and out of the docks, cut suddenly at places by the low hulls of the Cluthas as they dart from their dingy piers. It is very sombre, very work-a-day; to a modern Syntax (if his tour brings him so far), we fear, a little doleful. Yet it is all infinitely worth observing. There a swarming horse-ferry puffs and clanks along on its chain; in the first shipbuilding yard men are breaking up the pathway in front as they lay the ways for a launch; and in the next the cranes are swinging the ram of a battleship into its section. On the other bank a stout-bodied Canadian screw is discharging timber on the Yorkhill wharf to the cries of men and the rattle of derricks; further along, beside a panting workshop, an old passenger boat from the Outer Isles is at her spring toilet. Across the river crowds of workmen are fixing up the blocks round the Indian liner which has just come into the Prince's Dry Dock, and now looks a toy thing on a shelf, with little black figures scattered over its deck. Insistent tenements crowd round the docks at this point; there is no great Custom House to add a touch of dignity to its monotonous row of sheds; and the sky-line is broken only by the masts in Queen's and Prince's Docks, tall chimneys **Harbour** and a far spire.   On the Finnieston quay are **wonders** planted the biggest cranes of the harbour.   Here you may see the finishing stages of shipmaking in tremendous energy.   Huge boilers move in mid-air, funnels are being stepped, traction engines strain along with masses of machinery, workmen

" Paddy's Market "

toil up long gangways—everything is in motion, and to a different measure.   It is like looking into the works of a clock.   And beneath your feet there is more activity, a stream of traffic crossing below the Clyde from the one brick rotunda to the other by the harbour tunnel.   Here, also, the Finnieston elevating horse-ferry, with its moveable

"We've got
the ships" deck which defies the tide and is always at street
level, traverses the river in all its state. Thought-
ful people are divided in their admiration between
this ingenious construction and the other wonder
of the harbour—the tall Highland policeman you
may observe near the ferry entrance, directing, in
the politest of Hindustani, the little dark men
from the Indian liner on their way to the Old
Clothes Market. Both, it is believed, are unique.

The middle-aged Queen's Dock, with its single
sheds and slack hydraulic capstans, lies beside
you on the north side, and the modern Prince's
Dock, with its new equipment and its two-storey
sheds of brick on the other. A third basin,
Kingston Dock, which dates back to the days of
the sailing clippers, is situate nearer the city, on
the south side.

If you compare Glasgow with other large ports,
perhaps its most distinguishing feature is the comprehensive nature of its trading. The liner *de
luxe*, as Liverpool people understand her in
the "Oceanic" or the "Campania" or the "St.
Louis," is not to be seen on the narrow Clyde;
and the Cardiff man, accustomed to his miles
of coal traders, will find disappointment here;
still, if you were to spend a diligent morning
in the docks, you will find few types of the
British mercantile marine amissing. The Transatlantic passenger steamers of the Allan and
Anchor firms, the strange East-Coastish lines of
the Donaldson carriers ("lines like a hat-box," as

an old skipper had it), the queer-shaped turret Shipping ships of the Clan Company, which look as though they had swallowed much more cargo than they could digest, the big, bright-funnelled South American traders, bristling with derricks and samson-posts; the China Mutual steamers, with

Sailed Schooners
in the Queens Docks

their names in the script of Far Cathay on their bows; the Loch Line sailing ships, which clip Australian records every season as keen as any "greyhound of the Atlantic"; the four-masted Frenchman from New Caledonia, the teak carrier from Rangoon, the auxiliary screw laden with seal oil and skins from Harbour Grace, the nitrate barque from Chili, the City steamers from India

I

**The head of
the harbour**

and the Persian Gulf—you can find them all. Then
there are the squadrons of tramps which thrash
from Bilbao to the Clyde with ore and back again
with coal; the Italian fruit boats, the stout cross-
channel packets, the Highland steamers, and top-
sail schooners which congregate in the Kingston
Dock.

Returning to the river, you see on the south side
the general terminus of the railway mineral lines,
where more colliers swarm round the cranes.
From this point the sheds run up without a break
to where the vista is traced by the pleasant lines
of what man calls Gleska Brig. Above that a few
of the smaller fry find wharfage, but the harbour
practically ends at the bridge. In 1848, it is
true, the Examining Commissioner of the Tidal
Harbour Board put forward the brilliant idea in
his report that the real site for a harbour for large
vessels was not at Stobcross, but near the Custom
House and between the bridges. Yet, as the Clyde
Trustees pointed out, this plan had its difficulties.
For one thing the cost of acquiring the land was
too high, and large vessels with masts and funnels
hinged for the passage of Glasgow Bridge were, on
the whole, rare.

The head of the harbour is no more impressive
than its entrance. In place of the spacious
dignity, the delicate perspectives (and the storms)
of the wide Mersey, there is a fairway but 620 feet
at the widest point and 362 at the narrowest.
Where the Thames has its curious old warehouses

Baronscourt Bridge.

rising sheer from the waters, the intricate detail of its wharves, the touches of green at its old church-yards, with the outlines of St. Paul's tremendous over the city, we have a constant repetition of depressing sheds and tenements, the yellow chimney of the Clyde Trust, the dingy Sailors' Home with its globe tower, and (smoke permitting) the high lands to the north, and the façade of the railway hotel. Taking the port of Glasgow from dock to dock, we find the bald facts of shipping commerce squarely stated, nothing softened by the presence of old memorials, nor aught set down for decoration—" No picturesque nonsense here" (I have heard said); "a practical harbour, sir, constructed by business men for business men." _{placeholder}

But, with all due respect to the Clyde Trustees, you can't shut a glimpse of the picturesque out of any camp of industry, neither can you lock romance out of a harbour. Place where you will your electric cranes, your Deputy Harbour-masters, your two-storey sheds, a harbour is still what more than the melodramatists would call the Home of Romance, the beginning of far issues, the opening scene of many a drama that has rung down to the cries of the Furies, or on a silent, listed boat in a burning sea. Two men take their turn of a stumpy pen in a shipping office as they sign on as ship-mates in a voyage to New Zealand; last month they were steaming home from opposite ends of the earth. Behind the steel plating of that liner the good Lascar is praying to Allah, and Mahomet

[115]

Romance his Prophet, that he may acquire enough empty
marmalade jars in the smoky city to set up as
Sirkar at Ratnaghari; a joss stick is smoking in
some dark forecastle at Stobcross; a man with the
look of an engineer is hurrying through the turn-
stiles with a fairy wreath of South Sea coral
destined to lie in a Govan front parlour below
the portraits of the Scottish football team of 1899-
1900. Or, the dour little vista of a rainy dock
street is dignified suddenly and memorised by the
presence of two figures—a mother God-speeding
her son: stock situation as old and obvious in its
pathos as when his forebears put out with the
Great Adventurers; and now, as then, the lad has
eyes only for their pennant, fluttering and beckon-
ing at the mast head, above the driving harbour
smoke, the eternal emblem of romance—the Blue
Peter.

Fairfield Shipyard — Govan

V

Shipbuilding

A dignified OUR modern university may not impress
industry you, the cathedral you may never see (for
lack of a native able to lead you to

it); but our shipbuilding yards are a **The making** different matter. Before you are two days in the **of ships** city you are aware of their existence; and if their importance is a matter beyond you, at least you must be impressed by our belief in it. We believe, every Glasgow man of us, that our shipbuilding is a thing to be talked of, and a most honourable and dignified business to have for the chief industry of a city. Sheffield is known to the world for cutlery, Birmingham for pedlars' wares and nails and bullets, and Manchester for "Manchester goods." But Glasgow is the maker of ships, and her sons are proud of their seemly product. The Clyde builder may pride himself, too, on his achievement. Following no man, he hewed out a path for himself; borrowed no capital, but at his own door dug coal and iron and wrought up these into that modern wonder, the steamship. And through a century he counts his tale of triumphs from the "Comet" to the "Campania." Now and then, it is true, he had the wit to use the ideas of other men, to weld their inventions to his own purposes and to profit by their errors. But take him for all in all, he is the figure which dominates modern shipbuilding, the inspirer and pioneer to whom all other builders must bow, and without whom the glorious company of ships had shrunken to a half. The teachers of youth are very right; of more moment to Glasgow than

The "Comet" her other industries, her college, her cathedral, is the building of her ships.

If you glance at the history of the industry you find the Clyde's name writ large on every page. Sailing ships may be left out of account; they are part of an older scheme of things, and their building is now no man's special business. Still, if you insist on it, the Clyde can produce you whole sheaves of laurels gathered by her clippers, which have even sailed into the pages of literature, for was not the " Narcissus " herself "born in the thundering peal of hammer beating upon iron in black eddies of smoke under a grey sky on the banks of the Clyde?" We may say, without any straining of facts, that steam navigation was born on our river. For the first vessel constructed for the purpose of steaming in open water was that designed by Henry Bell, built by John Wood, of Port-Glasgow, launched into the Clyde in 1812, and christened the " Comet," because she flashed through water at a rate of nearly six miles an hour. No doubt there were earlier vessels of the kind—the small pleasure boat which, with Robert Burns on board, appeared to the wonder of beholders on Dalswinton Loch; Symington's other venture, the " Charlotte Dundas," which ran for a perilous season on the Forth and Clyde Canal, and (as American cousins would perhaps remind us) Fulton's " Clermont " of the Hudson.

But if these are to be counted, we may shift our
ground and aver that but for the discoveries of
a lank Greenock youth who came to Glasgow
at the age of eighteen, not one of them had ever
cleft water.

When steam propulsion had been shown to be
practicable, the next step was to make it cheap
enough for alliance with commerce, and in solving
this problem in economics the Clyde again
played chief part. Of first importance was the
invention of the marine compound engine, a
discovery which, by doubling the motive power
of ships, began a new epoch in steam navigation,
so much did it expand its possibilities and open
the way for further development. For stationary
engines the compound principle had been
employed for several years. John Elder, of
Fairfield, was the first to adapt it to marine
purposes. Using it in conjunction with the
surface condenser (originally introduced by
David Napier in 1822, but little applied till his
own time) he increased the pressure of steam
from about thirty to eighty pounds to the square
inch and reduced the coal consumption by almost
one-half. Another benefit we owe to Elder's
ingenuity was the modification of the compound
principle to screw-propelled vessels with inverted
engines, and it was this contrivance which led to
the screw supplanting the paddles for ocean
steaming. Compound engines permitted the

[119]

steam to be used twice; triple-expansion, which
came into use a few years later, forced it to do
duty a third time. This invention was introduced by Mr. Alexander Taylor, of Newcastle,
in 1882, but Dr. Kirk, who was one of the
partners of John Elder & Company, had been
experimenting on a similar contrivance at the
same time, and it was his model which was
applied to the Admiralty ships. A further com-
pounding was planned by Mr. Walter Brock, of
Denny & Company, in the form of quadruple-
expansion engines, which demanded as basis an
initial pressure of 180 pounds to the square
inch when the steam is first used as it comes
from the boiler. In the days of Henry Bell a
five pound pressure was considered something
uncanny. Thus, the Clyde engineer, bit by bit,
tightened his hold upon steam, and by his instant
embodiment in his work of these and other
inventions increased the prestige which Napier
and Denny had brought to his river.

While these important changes were made in
the engine room, the structure of the vessel itself
had altered greatly. The material changed from
wood to iron, then from iron to steel, and in
both cases our district has its claim ready as
innovator. A small vessel constructed on the
Monkland Canal about 1822 is generally set down
as the first vessel built of iron, and before the
paddle steamer "Windsor Castle," an eighteen-
knot racer of the 'sixties, was constructed by

Caird, of Greenock, there was no steel steamer
afloat. The case for the Clyde, as regards many
important structural improvements, need not,
perhaps, be pushed too far. From France came
mild steel as a material, and from England the
longitudinal and cellular bottom system and its
application to water-ballast; still, it was here
that these inventions were developed and turned
to their greatest use, and it was here that owners
came in the heyday of shipping when the best
in the market was wanted.

If you select the route in which fine workmanship and great speed are first necessities, the
Clyde's prestige is most clearly demonstrated.

The North Atlantic, it is agreed, is the royal
racecourse of maritime nations. Here the reward
in mail subsidies, big rates, and quickest of
returns awaits the successful, and here is Fame
in a pilot cutter with her loudest trumpet blowing. And to serve the Transatlantic service are
engaged in their highest form the art and practice of shipbuilding and marine engineering.
The engines of the "Sirius," first vessel to cross
the Atlantic under steam, were constructed by
Thomas Wingate, of Whiteinch. From 1840 to
1851, 1864 to 1872, 1880 to 1891, and 1892
to 1899 the Clyde-built steamers held the
supremacy of the Atlantic. It was the four
famous pioneer steamers of the Cunard line—
"Britannia," "Arcadia," "Caledonia," and
"Columba"—built on the river in 1840, and all

engined by Robert Napier, that by the speed
of their paddles first brought America within
fourteen days' distance of Europe. In 1863 the
"Scotia," constructed by Napier, made the first
passage of nine days; Tod & Macgregor's "City
of Rome" the first of eight days; Elder's
"Alaska" the first of seven; Thompson's "City
of Paris" the first of six; and although that old
Clyde decoration, "the blue ribbon of the Atlantic,"
now adorns the log of a liner made in Germany,
the five days' passage is yet to make. If the
Clyde builder is resting on his oars for the
moment, it is not that his skill has failed, but
that he has not been bidden to beat the newest
Germans. The brains and the hammers are still
on the Clyde, but as long as British shipowners
reckon small coal consumpts far above records
he must bide his time. When the day comes the
five days' passage will, without doubt, be added to
his other laurels.

If for the fleeting moment, of course, the Clyde
is somewhat overshadowed in certain respects,
if her record for building the fastest ship has
gone one airt, and for building the biggest ship
another, she still stands unapproached and alone
in the magnitude and catholicity of her undertakings.

It is the distinction of the Clyde shipyards that
they can build any kind of vessel from a trawler
to a battleship. The builders have the skill and
experience, and the yards have the appliances

which are required for any type of war vessel, trading vessel, or pleasure craft. Elsewhere you may find—but not often—that in a given year more ships of a certain class were built than on the Clyde. Belfast and Stettin, for instance, are at the moment undoubtedly ahead of the Clyde in building great passenger steamers; but it is only here that you see every kind and manner of ship on the stocks. In the philosophy of Mr. Squeers, when you have spelt the name of any kind of craft from d-r-e-d-g-e-r to b-a-t-t-l-e-s-h-i-p you may go to Glasgow and see it a-building.

Thus if you would establish a service of weekly steamers, say, to the sea-coast of Bohemia, your fleet, with their twin-screws and six-decks, may be laid down and delivered within the year; or if you are a millionaire seeking an 8000-ton yacht that will float on a six-foot draught, " so that if it was ordainit to be stickit, it would be stickit in shallow water"; or if you are a romantic Syndicate, desiring a boat to dredge the Spanish Main for treasure; or the simple inventor of a perpetual motion gearing which (in a suitable ship) will let a British owner sail nearer the wind than ever, why, then, the Clyde has, in one or other of its yards, the builder you need; and for a price you may have your heart's desire. If you come it will be in good company, for all the world comes here to buy; and if cost is not the cheapest, at any rate all

The Clyde and the Admiralty the world profits sufficiently by the purchase to come again a-shopping. So that " Clyde-built," you may say, is engraved on the nameplate of every type (well, nearly every type) of craft that rides water, salt or fresh. Peace and war alike bring grist to our river's mill ; for peace brings orders for merchantmen, and war (or the fear of war) orders for ships to protect them. And so the two kinds of craft may be seen sitting cheek by jowl in the Govan shipyards.

The honour of presenting the first Clyde-built steamer to the British Navy on the open sea belongs to Dumbarton. The Dennys had built a boat named the " Marjory," and had sent her under her own steam to her purchaser on the Thames. On her voyage, it is related, she fell in with a British fleet on the Downs, and vastly amazed the officers and men of His Britannic Majesty. Many of them—like the Kirkintilloch saddler—recording his impression of the "Charlotte Dundas"—

> "Thocht frae hell she had cam hither
> A-privateering."

Others thought her a fire-ship from France despatched before her time. But to solve all doubts she was hailed and her port demanded. " Dumbarton, on the Clyde," came the proud reply, and in this manner Clyde shipbuilding and the Royal Navy made the first bow of their long and honourable acquaintance.

Some time elapsed before the importance of the new power laid to their hand came home to the Lords Commissioners of the Admiralty, but since Robert Napier astounded the drowsy dockyard mandarins by constructing an iron floating battery for the Crimea in the space of three months, the Clyde has no reason to complain of its share in the making of the British Navy, nor the British Navy of the Clyde's contributions. Old shipbuilding hands, who squabble o' nights in riverside taverns over bygone days, and piece together ancient Atlantic records, will tell you that it is now forty years since they can remember a time when there was no British warship on our stocks or in our fitting-out basins. The tardy supply of armoured plate, and the generous views held by the Clyde workmen on the subject of holidays and Admiralty "ways of doin'," rob the river of many a bonnie order that, without doubt, should be hers ; but even when, *pour encourager les autres*, an eminent firm was suspended from the contract list, the Clyde figured highest in the Naval Estimates, and more particularly in the Supplementary Estimates. Without her aid the First Lord would be hard pressed to execute a presentable Naval Programme, for our river is always counted on for two-fifths of the contract work. Last year the Admiralty paid over two millions to the Clyde builder, this being an amount larger by some hundred thousand pounds than that which came

War vessels the way of the Thames and Barrow establishments
put together. In the present year it is proposed
to lay out nearly five and a half millions, and of
that sum about half goes to the Clyde. The
purchases have included every type of vessel
that figures in the Navy List—first-class cruisers
of the three grades, such as the 14,000-ton " Good

A Cruiser at Fairfield

Hope" and "Leviathan" now in the river,
the 12,000-ton "Bacchante," and the 9800-ton
"Bedford" and "Monmouth" that you may see
on the Govan and Fairfield stocks; second-class
cruisers, the last to be handed over being the
"Hyacinthe" in 1900; gunboats, torpedo boat
destroyers, Admiralty tugs, and all the other

mailed gauntlets that are required for hands that rule the waves. And the Clyde war vessels, like her merchantmen, sail under many flags; a very considerable squadron could be organised from the units she has contributed to other navies. Considering only those in commission, there is the Japanese battleship " Asahi," 15,200 tons, built at Clydebank last year, which, but for the fact that she has a sister-ship, would be the largest war vessel in the world; and the " Chizoda," a cruiser of 2452 tons. America has the " Scipio," 3385 tons, built by Denny; the " Mayflower," 2690 tons, built by Thompson; and the " Sterling," 5663 tons, built by Duncan; Russia the " Moskoa" and " Opit," of 3050 tons and 3920 tons, both built at Fairfield; Portugal the " Africa," 2990 tons, and " India," 1200 tons, built by Denny; Holland the " Havik " and the " Zeemeuw," 350 tons each, all built at Fairfield; Turkey the " Azizah," " Orkanuh," and " Os-maneh," each of 6400 tons, built at Fairfield; France, Spain, and Italy have at one time or another purchased war craft of varying power from our builders, while most of the little South American Republics have a Clyde gunboat.

The prestige of the Clyde merchantman is, perhaps, not so all-apparent as it was in the days when the Nordeutscher Lloyd started their great enterprise with seven Fairfield vessels, or when the Compagnie Generale Transatlantique purchased second-hand Clyde liners to establish a French

Clyde liners service of the first class ; but with all respect
to Stettin and Belfast, it is not yet eclipsed.
The Clyde yards, which have fought in the van
of shipbuilding progress since the conquest of
steam began, have records to inspire and traditions to uphold, and despite pneumatic tools
and trade unions, there still lingers a kind of
esprit de corps among the builders and their men,
a belief in the yard and its destinies. The practical outcome of this is the famed " Clyde finish,"
which means the final touch of craftsmanship
applied to its most scientific end, and although
some allege it to be something of a fetish, it yet
weighs with shipowners, and the shipowner is not
a man of sentiment. It is said to mean the perfect
articulation of parts making for durability and
smoothness in working, and all this spells
economy. At anyrate the half-dozen Clyde fore-
men who first crossed the North Sea to teach the
German operatives their business, say they did not
leave their secret at Stettin ; and the Clyde
builder will prove to you that the building of the
world's great steam yachts—which demands the
highest excellence of workmanship—is not done
at Belfast.

The *élite* of the great liners, you will find, first
smelt water on the dingy Clyde. Here were
launched the famous Cunarders, from the
" Britannia " to the " Lucania," the best
pick of the Orient liners (including the
" Ophir," which it would be now high

treason to dispute, is the most resplendent **Passenger**
merchantman afloat), of the Castle, the Union, **steamers**
the Pacific, British India, P. & O., Royal
Mail, Hamburg-American — in fact of every
company of note, if you except the White
Star—a corporation which grieves the Clyde man
to the heart by launching elsewhere the biggest
vessels on earth every other year.

But apart from Clyde "finish" in the liners,
it exists indisputably in the other branches of the
industry. The Calais-Dover service, which has
the most fastidious *clientèle* on earth ; the Queen-
borough and Flushing, Havre and Dieppe,
Liverpool and Isle of Man, Tilbury and Boulogne
(where plies with her six thousand passengers the
Fairfield-built "La Marguerite," the biggest
paddle steamer afloat), and the Isle of Wight and
Bristol Channel routes, all depend almost exclu-
sively on boats from Fairfield, Clydebank, and
Dumbarton. Thus the traveller is not surprised
to find that the fleet of passenger steamers on the
Clyde is the fastest and best in existence, or to
learn that when it is considered advisable to withdraw a boat from the Clyde she finds a respectful
welcome on the Thames. As early as the 'sixties
we had an 18-knot steamer on these waters, and
when the American Civil War broke out, and
Europe was searched for fast vessels to " run the
blockade " of the Federal fleet into the ports of the
South, the Clyde, in the " Rothesay Castle,"
" Kelpie," " Falcon," and " Flamingo," supplied

K   [129]

Passenger steamers

the most famous. Nowadays you can travel from Ardrossan to Arran at the rate of twenty-one miles an hour in the "Glen Sannox." As showing at once the exploitation of Clyde shipbuilding and the importance of the Glasgow man's time—even on holiday—it may be mentioned that this amazing steamer, built purely for a thirty-mile passage, has the dimensions of an early Cunarder. And it is not only Europe that the Clyde provides with river steamers. Every year the alligators on the Amazon are startled by a new wonder in twin-screw awning-deckers. When the Rajah of Sarawak puts along the shore it is in his Clyde-built paddle boat; and after toiling through the swamps and forests of Africa the traveller to the great lakes will find the Clyde steamer and Broomielaw accent of her engineer borne over their mysterious depths.

"Tramps"

Coming to the cargo boat proper, and her near relation, the "composite liner," we find they can be produced in every class from the 14,000-ton "Saxonia," of Clydebank, to the little East Coast trawlers which a Govan firm is said to be able to knock together while the buyer takes a fairly long stroll round the yard. That useful, hard-working class of ship which Mr. Kipling has likened to a "shuttle," but which the plain, unassuming man calls "tramp," provides the bulk of the Clyde's output, but, as one trader resembles another most mathematically, there is little to be said on that head save that the Clyde builder has yet failed

to unite carrying capacity with supreme ugliness **Dredgers and others**
of line in the way that will move your stevedore
to tears of joy as he sights a new East Coaster
drawing nigh his sheds.

There remain " specialities," and the greatest of
these is the dredger. Every type of these pioneers
of shipping commerce can be purchased in either
of our two yards which are concerned wholly in
their making and perfecting. It was Simons
& Company, of Renfrew, who set the first steam
dredger a-working in 1824, and this alert old
firm last year in " La Puissante," a stern-well
construction of 4000 tons, built for the Suez
Canal, put into the water the largest and most
powerful of its class in the world. Were space
permitted for eulogies on stern-wheel steamers,
vehicular ferries, pontoons, and barges, the picture
of the Clyde output would be near completion.
A few types, it is true, we have still to add—
vessels for Arctic exploration and submarine warfare—before the Clyde can claim to be the ency-
clopædia of modern shipbuilding, but the first will
come in time if the North Pole holds out, and when
the second is no longer caviare to the Admiralty, it
shall find a place in our menu. To show that
the Clyde shipbuilder keeps in the front of his
times, the latest trick in marine engineering and
river turbine-motor passenger steamer that is to
run at least twenty-three miles an hour, and could,
but for the danger to passengers' hats, add another
ten, was launched at Dumbarton this year. And

The first steam yacht

it is not only such old-fashioned problems as sailing the waters that are confronted here. The Clyde has an eye on the future, and in the same workshop is building an air-ship for a Spanish gentleman, which, we are assured, will fulfil a more practical purpose than flying from one *chateau d'Espagne* to another.

The construction of steam yachts has been associated with the river from the infancy of steam propulsion. To old Robert Napier came all men of his time with advanced notions in naval architecture, and to this great builder, in 1829, came a notable English yachtsman, Thomas Hopeton Smith, of Tednorth, with a desire to possess a pleasure yacht driven by steam. Napier reduced the squire's plans to practice, and built for him a 400-ton boat, the first vessel of its kind ever put in the water. During the succeeding twenty years he built eight yachts for the adventurous Englishman, who, it is said, lost the confidence of his wife and the Royal Yacht Squadron's membership in return for the honour of pioneering the steam yacht. The largest of his fleet, a vessel of 700 tons and 30 horse-power, named the " Fire King II.," he offered to race from Dover round the Eddystone Lighthouse and back against anything afloat for a wager of five thousand guineas, but no one could be found to take up his challenge. The " Fire King II." cut a great figure in her day, and as the steam yacht grew in favour among the restricted class concerned, the Clyde

was installed as builder in ordinary and in extraordinary to the great ones of the earth. British
royalty, it is true, have not yet come north for
the State barge, and thus you must be prepared
to find on the Clydeside something apart from
sympathy when the mishaps of the new " Victoria
and Albert " are mentioned; but, on the other
hand, it was here the Czar of All the Russias
ordered his celebrated " Livadia," the most auto-
cratic and expensive pleasure vessel — always
excepting the said " Victoria and Albert "—ever
constructed. This remarkable boat was built by
John Elder & Company, of Fairfield, to the
designs of Admiral Popoff of the Russian Navy.
Her distinguished designer, who is stated to have
invented a battleship to rotate on its own axis,
intended the vessel to remain perfectly steady
in all weathers, and the " Livadia " was planned
with a construction underneath, which was to
act as a breakwater to the hull proper. One
expert has called her turbot-shaped, another held
that her lines were those of a cup placed on an
inverted saucer, and another that the mock turtle
originally suggested her shape, but in any case
she was the only vessel which made billiards at
sea seem at all feasible. She was 235 feet
long, 153 feet broad, and had a draught of 6 feet
6 inches; her gross tonnage measured 7700, and
her yacht measurement, according to Thames Club
rules, showed an aggregate of 11,600 tons. For
her construction the Czar had to foot a bill of

[133]

The latest yachts

nearly £300,000. The launch was a great affair, and is still remembered on the Clyde as a red-letter event. Nor will it be forgotten soon that on that day Glasgow was publicly referred to, and by a Grand Duke of Russia, as "the centre of the intelligence of England."

The revolution in naval architecture that the "Livadia" was expected to forerun, however, has not yet become prominent, but this we must put down to the fact that she still remains ahead of any practical use we can make of her lesson. The Clyde's recent contributions to steam yachting have taken more the form of ideal liners than experiments in hydro-dynamics. The American millionaire, to be sure, has shown a few idiosyncrasies in ideas of what is what in a floating hotel. Mr. Gordon Bennett's "Lysistrata," for instance, dispenses with masts, and has a cycling track on deck, while at her bow electric eyes (after the Chinese theory, "if ship no got eyes, no can see; if no can see, no can go") glare balefully on mere work-a-day craft. But compared with Czar Alexander's revolutionary ideas, these are mild novelties, indeed. Particularly impressed by the Clyde article, the American dollar lord for the last ten years has gone nowhere else when he would outdo the sovereigns of the earth in maritime grandeur and dignity. Clydebank has built the "Mayflower" and the "Wahma," each a vessel of 1800 tons; Inglis, the "Varuna," 1564

tons; and Scott, of Greenock, the "Tuscarova," **The latest**
580 tons. Two others, the "Lysistrata" and the **yachts**
"Marguerita," which lay in the river together at
the beginning of the year, commanding universal
respect, if only by the mere fact that they cost
a quarter of a million between them, gave to the
Clyde the last words on the subject of steam-yacht
construction.

In conclusion one may add that the Clyde
produced for the world's shipping last year
296 vessels, representing an aggregate tonnage
of about 487,000 tons, and of these 54
vessels were for Dutch, Austrian, Spanish,
German, South American, Japanese, United
States, French, Russian, Norwegian, and Colonial
owners. Included in the list are a first-class
cruiser, a nineteen-knot troopship, torpedo boat
destroyers, whose contract speed is thirty knots,
two 12,000-ton "composite" liners, Red Star,
P. & O., Allan, and Anchor liners, fast paddle
steamers for cross-channel service, tramps, sailing
ships, dredgers, and the two yachts for
millionaires.

VI

Architecture

In accounting Glasgow heedless of her looks, **Stone—its**
and contemptuous of effect, one must guard **virtues**
against the unfairness of sweeping generalisations.

Its monotony   For, undeniably, Glasgow's appearance on the
whole is the most consistently dignified of any
industrial city save London.   Building here is
everywhere of a certain massiveness and weight,
though, perhaps, in saying so much one is making
a virtue of necessity.   The cost of building in
Glasgow is high, and a house must needs be
built well and solidly from the very outset; it
is never, or rarely, altered, and so our streets
lack the improvisations that enliven by their
variety and whimsicality the perspective of London
or Liverpool, and afford endless interesting " bits "
for the picturesque sketcher, who never cranes
his neck in Glasgow streets.   From the day it
is built until the day it is demolished the Glasgow
house receives no attention or adornment.   Spring
surprises no painters on tall ladders making our
façades look French and fine, or picking out
with neat, white lines a stone jointing that doesn't
exist, or painting the rose-brick doubly red after
the absurd fashion of London.   Our stone is *real*
stone, and—there is No Stucco.   The thing results
in a terrible uniformity, unrelieved by a single
note of colour.   The gaudy signs which give the
Strand its flaunting character, or the tints which
make the slender tall slips of painted, flower-clad
houses in the London West End appear to Scots-
men as foreign as Florence, are here quite wanting.
We do nothing, though sometimes nature comes
to our aid and enlivens our blank façades with
touches of green; but this is only in the suburbs

or where the parks are. So you may find in such **The high average** places as Scotstounhill and Bearsden pretty boulevard streets; but sobriety, not to say downright gloom, is the key-note elsewhere. Modern brick becomes so shabby in a town that stucco and paint and flower-boxes are quite necessary alleviations. Stone, on the other hand, is accounted so dignified a material that in theory it requires no adjuncts of any sort to effect a beautiful result. But, alas, we reckon without smoke, and universal dulness is the penalty we pay for belief in unadorned stone. Our consolation we find in this, that although the fresh paint and flowers of Mayfair make it a gayer and pleasanter place than Kelvinside, yet brick and stucco and musty paint make immense tracts of London horrible with a frowsiness that is happily impossible in Glasgow. Yet, if it is true that we never sink to very great depths, it is unfortunately as true that we never rise to very great heights. Glasgow might be defined as a High Average, with much in it that an architect would dismiss from notice as good family pudding. There are whole districts in the Northern and Eastern suburbs of woeful monotony—street lengths ruled into pigeon-holes for working families. But though the giant uniformity of these districts is not without a certain impressiveness when seen through the glasses of memory, one has a pride in knowing that there are streets upon streets in our town

Renaissance without a building in them that is mean or undignified. Yet the town has suffered in its architecture from being, not a royal and aristocratic capital, but the home of traders. There has been no wilful personality at work in it; the rights of each citizen have to be considered too much to allow of great clearances for the

spacious site of a nobly proportioned building. " Canniness " is an admirable virtue in a man or a municipality, but it chills achievement in architecture. No one but a Hausmann can mend the matter of site, but in the proportions and style of the buildings themselves it would seem that " canniness " is giving way to a worthy civic emulation among the great mercantile The "new" art companies. The last few years have seen a change come over the town; to-day the eye is uplifted at every turn by great picturesque erections of red stone that are adding a kind of jocund quality to the life of our streets, like good-humoured red-faced giants in ranks of rather pallid men. Within a radius of half a mile from the Exchange there is much that is balanced and

Duke Street Gaol

well relieved, and the newest comers are breaking up the skyline with an almost startling variety of profile, while the sparing use of the emphasis of detail upon wide, tranquil spaces lends it the sudden brilliance of a good "attack" in music. There is to be noted, also, a growing tendency to accentuate the constructional lines. The style has become not only simpler, but more varied, and almost everywhere the belief that

**"Greek"
Thomson** honesty lies at the root of good art is refreshingly
evident. Some few things here and there show
a weedy, " arty " influence, and in certain places
the strange idea seems to obtain that the vegetable is the architect's pattern. But it must be
said, on the whole, that architecture is distinctly
promising in the West of Scotland. Where the
good seed first took root it is hard to say.
Throughout the city there are a few buildings of
the great classic age that are extremely dignified.
Adam's Royal Infirmary is one, and its sensitively
felt proportions have no doubt been among the
things that helped. St. George's Church, in
Buchanan Street, is rather weighty too, and the
old Justiciary Court at the entrance to the Green
seems like a page from Méryon's sketch-book, so
intently do the little prison windows under the
shadow of the cornice regard you.

These are works of the early nineteenth century,
and after them came the nondescript, dubious
things that choke our streets with dulness.
Perhaps the first Glasgow architect of the new
era (in which styles are arbitrarily chosen and
combined, and depend for effect more on artistic
feeling than on correct classic detail) was " Greek "
Thomson, a man consumed with a passion for
bizarre arrangements of Greek and Egyptian
ornament. He was a contemporary of crinolines
and " Mid-Victorian Art," and much of his work
smacks of old-fashioned " antique," but he brought
together some effects so novel and personal, that

a fevered admiration for him invariably attacks James Sellars every young enthusiast that enters a Glasgow architect's office. And such a work as the Great Western Terrace in Kelvinside almost persuades one to enlist under his flag. The sureness and precision in its simple arrangement say their say with the absoluteness of a masterpiece. Yet the thing is like a divinely proportioned factory. In Union Street there is a work from the same hand, of a very different kind—a sumptuous cornice that seems in the dullest weather to be playing with a light and shade, entrapped, some brilliant day, amid the many facets of its rich members. The most original church in Glasgow—a little domed one in a back street of Queen's Park—is his, and the great thing that perpetually astonishes the travellers on their car-tops proceeding along Bothwell Street—a façade that rises imperious as an Italian cathedral from a low muddle of workshop roofs—is his also. James Sellars, an architect who belonged to our own time, probably helped the modern revival of mercantile architecture more than any other man ; his New Club in West George Street is a faultlessly graceful piece of work. St. Andrew's Halls, standing in an open space with the verandah down, would be hailed as a wonderful discovery by the people who pass it to-day without a look. Sellars will long be remembered as a designer of ironwork—no stock pattern would satisfy him ; his grilles, panels, and gates are wonders of grace and suppleness.

Among its public buildings Glasgow has none that is quite as satisfactory as the St. George's Hall of Liverpool. But we must remember that we have no city square to afford the same imposing site. The greatest we have is that occupied by the University, though not in the way one could dream of. The building is the work of a man who was competent enough, but who was a scholar rather than an instinctive artist. We should be proud to have a house designed by him, feeling sure that it would be a thing of dignity. But the task which was set him by this great site and the memories of our ancient University, was beyond his powers, and "the classic pile on Gilmorehill" is not as wonderful as the guide-books say. As the crown of a considerable eminence, it lacks a great movement, a notable gesture. Its hundred little prickly turrets confuse the eye and distract the attention; the tower itself has been described by a youthful critic as "a needle stuck in a cork," and certainly a heaviness in the building, which is sufficient to be dull and not weighty enough to be impressive, combines with a certain scantiness in the proportions of the spire to produce this impression. It is doubtful if Scott realised the exceptional position which his building was to occupy; something in the long lines of the front elevation suggest that he did, but the side elevations seem to be apologies for usurping a vantage-ground. There is a fatal desultoriness in the composition, and the whole has the look of a work that has grown too great for the hands of the designer. The detail is harmonious and well considered, and is the work of a scholar, and yet the reflection one is left with is this—that for a great national effort such as the building of our University, a man is required who is more than merely competent. And when we recollect that another opportunity of the kind may not occur in ten generations, we have a right to be irritated. If we are asked what *should* have been, naturally we find ourselves on more difficult ground ; but this much at least might be said, that to add little mock heights to a height that is already great is a contradiction of well-established principles ; the explosive little turrets everywhere give the lie to the gently swelling hill on which they rise, and nullify it into a great garden plot. Had the design been some long classic building lying along the hill-top, crowning it, then the hill would have its due importance, and the University would have seemed a temple to go up into.

Equal with the University in interest are the Municipal Buildings in George Square. The style is classic, the general appearance is imposing, and sufficiently suggestive of a great city's Palace of Common Good. The elevation to the Square is not, however, quite successful. The three storeys under the pediment are almost identical in treatment and size, and the eye,

The Municipal Buildings

Its tower wandering in search of some distinctive feature, finds rest nowhere. The entrance is insignificant, the order missing its effect by being used so liberally elsewhere. The screen walls where the figures sit are well arranged, and the domed

Municipal Buildings
& Bank of Scotland

corners are quite gracefully designed, and form perhaps the most satisfactory parts of this elevation; the rusticated basement is a little meagre and diffident. The thinness of effect in the whole façade, which may be owing to the

smallness of the order used, makes the whole The Cathedral
composition appear timid, and wanting in openness
and relief.   The tower, when seen from a
distance, has a certain fineness, but above the
cornice, where it breaks into the round, there
is detail that fatigues the eye. The inevitableness
of art is scarcely to be found in it.   The side
elevations of the buildings are much more satisfactory, and the treatment of the George Street
entrance very nearly merits 'unqualified praise.
The scale of the orders is increased here with so
great a gain in dignity that one is sorry that the
front to the Square is not here where this is, and
this open to the Square. Of the marble staircase
within the buildings it is not the part of a
friend of architecture to speak.

It is a proof of the waywardness of these
notes that no mention has yet been made of the
ancient Cathedral. Truth to say, it is so far
from our midst and so seldom in our thoughts,
that of the citizens many have never seen it,
and most have never stepped to the echoes in its
marvellous crypt. For the man on 'Change it
has no existence, and one may take it for certain
that he never was there, unless he attended
in his capacity of Bailie or Councillor at a rare
official " kirking " of the Corporation.   It is impossible to deny that the Cathedral in these days
is badly hit.   The once considerable eminence
upon which it stands has been made utterly insignificant to-day by the diversion of the sacred trout

L.

The Molendinar
Burn

stream Molendinar from its "rocky gorge" to **The Cathedral** an underground sewer, and by the levelling up of the valleys around it. No one is to blame, for the Molendinar, apparently, fell of itself into its present low estate, helplessly, without agency —as Tolstoi says that battles are lost or won. It became unbearable, and was put away underground—that is its history, its epitaph. Perhaps its old neighbour, the Cathedral, will one day see itself disposed of by a process as summary. As it is, it looks irritated by the continual pointing that robs the stone of its effect. The tall chimney stalks stand round it, an implacable cordon, as though bent on smeeking it out; behind it the graveyard of the Necropolis becomes every year more like broken glass crowning a Brobdignagian wall; in front of it a great expanse of poor's-house granolithic (by courtesy called Cathedral Square) provides a platform for the atheist, the evangelist, or the "boss union-smasher"; and across this space, on the site of the Arch-bishop's Palace, are now the close-mouths of Castle Street, and its windows are outraged by the vilest stained glass that ever came out of Germany. Truly the Cathedral of Glasgow is fallen on evil days. Yet it still means a haven, a Holy Place, in the wilderness of the East End; and to enter its gaunt nave and climb down the ancient stairs and (till you find your prison eyes) fumble in the dark and think of the age that hewed these stones, the age to which light and clearness were nothing, and only an emotion mattered—to do this is to be rid of much intolerableness in the life of modern Glasgow, and to be at rest at " Founder's Tomb." I can never bring myself to pronounce coldly on its architecture ; the spot is too strange and sacred for that. But travellers have given their word for it that the crypt is unique in Britain. After the Cathedral, the finest church in Glasgow is that of Blythswood Parish, in Bath Street. Its spire is almost a miracle of beautifully modulated members, and it springs from a stately street with the happiest grace.

There remain to be considered the Government buildings in Glasgow, and in this connection the chronicle is of very small beer. You see at once that the town has no official sanction for being the Second City in the Empire, for the Government Buildings are patched, and shabby, and meagre. The Post Office, a great, dull, staring place, is suburban when compared with that of Manchester or Edinburgh or Liverpool. And the Custom House is a solemn little thing, placed, not as in Dublin or Greenock, on an open quay which affords a promenade to observers of the harbour life, but in an out-of-the-way corner which only highly-trained civil servants can readily find.

But the city, as well as the Government, can fritter away ornamental opportunities, as Park Terrace shows. The buildings are admirable, and seem from almost any point to crown the **Municipal Art** hill, but the great staircase leading up to Park Church is quite spoiled for lack of openness. Had it led with the same noble flight of steps from the Prince of Wales' Bridge to the guns in the park, it had been as gallant a piece of architecture as the famous stairway in Verona.

Every city has the Albert Memorial it deserves, and the People's Palace is ours—a sad bungle of a worthy and honest idea. The part of Glasgow most like a desert is the Green, and so, to educate the masses and light them along the straight path of taste, the Palace was erected there, in the hope that people of sensibility would never see it. And the Corporation doubtless were proud of the trump card they played in closing it on Sundays against any wandering critic from another town, whom the dulness of the city might drive eastwards in search of exercise for his judgment. In the East End the Corporation was hardly on its mettle, but at Kelvingrove it made an effort, like Mrs. Dombey, and the new Art Galleries were born. No British municipality has erected so important a palace of art, and one could wish that this one deserved better the praises of the discerning. The interior may be all that is promised, but the outline has neither breadth nor majesty. True, the glittering hydra-headed Exhibition does it no reverence, and the judgment can hardly be absolute till that is removed; but

Iron Steeple

meanwhile it is architecture looking worried in Municipal Art a hundred different ways.

Yet, lest one is thought to be captious, the æsthetic debt which one owes to the Corporation may be here acknowledged. We are thankful for the loving (though recent) attention to the Corporation Galleries, the courageous purchase of Whistler's portrait of Carlyle, the decoration of the Banqueting Hall in the Municipal Buildings, the provision of municipal green-houses, and the care for the parks. And if the wandering critic from the South is disposed to smile at the meagre list, let him look about him in his own city, at the new panels of the London Royal Exchange, at the city collections of Manchester and Liverpool, and he will acknowledge that Glasgow cannot look to other towns for leading and light.

"In wi' the hen, Maggie.   Here comes the Glesca keelies."—
                                            West Country saying.

Royal Exchange Place

Part III

GLASGOW OF FICTION

I

The City Man

GLASGOW, like most towns given over to industry and commerce, has no leisured class. Some of the inhabitants do, indeed, contend that the class exists and contains thirty-one persons, who are professors at Gilmorehill. But this is an absurd contention, for if you include professors, how are you to treat the officials of the Board of Trade or of the Custom House, or even lieutenants of police? No, if the class exists in Glasgow it contains only nine-and-twenty persons, and these are not professors at all, but infantry officers stationed at Maryhill Barracks. And this is why the military man, whom, of a summer afternoon, you recognise by his flannels, his straw hat, and

Men of leisure

Men of
leisure
(falsely so
called)

his fox-terrier, has an air so wearied and listless.
With the other leisured men in the town he
may have dined every night since the regiment
came to Maryhill; now, on this pleasant day,
he is just a little tired of them and would almost
give his dog to any new person of the class who
could help him to air it. Think of it! Alone
of 750,000 people, he of the straw hat and
flannels has no "job."

No doubt there are others who are leisured
against their will; the business or professional
man, for instance, who is still on the stocks, the
waiters in Drury Street who are out of work,
the student who, as the decades roll over his head,
is turning "chronic." But to avoid being stared
at, a man of this stamp adopts at the least the
habits of the occupied, and then, like the
Sergeant at Law—

> Nowher so besy a man as he ther nas,
> And yet he seemed besier than he was.

The unashamedly leisured are the military man
and his rare twin brother the Oxford undergraduate in Glasgow for vacation.

Now, this character of the Glasgow man as one
having a job may be read by him who runs.
It affects dress, manners, habits, even expression. Thus, existing more for use than ornament,
the Glasgow man has small regard for the delicate
niceties of dress. He clothes himself for work,
and wears tweeds which have an air of being

[154]

worth their price. If he should bestow pains on his clothes and do their maker infinite credit, depend upon it, the very rarity of his caprice will earn him the title of "Tailor's Block." But even the most modest person respects what he has purchased, and thus in our uncertain climate he will wear his trousers turned up and will carry an umbrella, and these two habits are said to be the stigmata of the Glasgow man, revealing his origin even in the Outer Hebrides. Until he has "arrived" he rarely (except to funerals) wears a tall hat, unless indeed he is a professional man, and then if he is a lawyer it may sit on his head more as a badge of his calling than as a harmonious element in his colour scheme. Very often he hangs it in a cupboard before leaving his office, and should he chance to spend the next day a-golfing, his clerks will play charades with it in his private room. It is of a piece with his character that he refuses in business hours to be seen on the street with a stick in his hand. So to be seen would occasion the oddest surmises among his friends, the chief that he was leaving his office for good at a strangely early hour, or that he was a wedding guest. He might even seem to be a stranger passing through Glasgow on his way to the West Highlands. In Edinburgh, on the other hand, where appearance, not time, is money, a stick is carried even by the junior apprentice delivering a letter.

The plain, unassuming man

His gait and expression

Further, the Glasgow man walks quickly, without attention to gait or carriage. He swings his body, even his arms, and sometimes walks on his heels as being nearest the ground. But no one takes offence at this. People are all too busy, and if our friend has the air of being bound for an appointment of importance, every Glasgow man would congratulate him on having so good a reason for his haste. Be his gait never so crab-like, no one will chaff him. Why, after all, should one, if the man gets there? In a metropolis where conventions are inherited it may be different, but here where the people who observe the conventions are those who made them, appearances, unless they collide with a reasonable etiquette, matter not one straw.

If now, from clothes and carriage, you pass to faces, your evidence multiplies that the Glasgow man is a man of occupation. The faces are intelligent rather than handsome, alert and intent rather than gay, more conspicuous for character than breeding. Merriment is not common, yet neither is boredom. It is a sedate people that you see, having itself well under control, aware of its aims and pursuing them without swerving. The vagrant eye is not often seen. Our friend knows his town too well to be attracted greatly by what passes in the streets. He has something else to think about. Yet do not imagine that he looks listless or wearied like the military man, and perhaps unhappy into the bargain. He is simply undemonstrative, and having an object and scope for his activity, he depends for his contentment less on his outward impressions than one who has neither.

The typical Glasgow man whom you see in the street uniting all these characteristics in his person is not the merchant prince with sons at Harrow, the professional man, nor the great shipbuilder or engineer, but is a little grey, wiry

Ingram Street

man in plain clothes and a square felt hat. He has a good-going business, which is the source, if not of a fortune, at least of a competence. He lives in the suburbs, probably in the South Side; his wife is plump and commonplace and cheerful, his daughter quite pretty, his son at college " coming out for a doctor " and writing decadent verses for the magazine. He himself is the salt of the middle-class with all its virtues and

His limita-
tions

limitations. His face is full of the character
which brought him success; shrewdness, resolved-
ness, tenacity, energy, canniness, steadiness,
and sobriety—all these then are imprinted
upon it indelibly. Withal it is a kindly face
and belongs to one who is without pretension
and deserves the epithet which his friends give
him, of a "plain, unassuming man."

If you call at his office you will find that he
meets you with a simple and quiet directness
which brings you quickly to the point, and when
that is reached, bows you as quickly to the door.
Of the patron's airs or of servility there has not
been a trace. You have seen a typical Scot,
independent, cautious, shrewd, and "decent." A
man, you say, easy to get on with. He is clearly
of the people. In England in the same class
he would be vulgar and strident. Here he is
saved from that by his quietness and reserve.
He is very intelligent and far from ignorant.
He can state a case clearly and argue with point
and force, and he has, within limits, the open
mind. But he has many and obvious limitations.
In matters lying outwith the common province
he lacks interest. He is practically minded.
Imagination disturbs him not; nor do the arts
come nigh him. Very likely he admires "The
Doctor" and all the pictures that are bad. He
(or, to be fair, his wife) may even confuse
Tannhäuser with San Toy, and ask if new songs
are in it this winter. And in music, his taste is

[158]

for melodies that set his toes in motion. Never-theless, he is a worthy man and the sound core of the city's inhabitants.

Glasgow's motto: "Push"

In the lower ranks his counterpart, whom you see less of in the street, is the young shopkeeper. A bright wee man this, blazing with ambition and business instinct. He can read and write, but is almost illiterate. He has every prejudice that can lodge in a man's mind. But he works without ceasing, and is already on the road to success. At the beginning he was a railway despatch clerk at so-and-so-little a week. Then he married and, borrowing the capital, commenced haberdasher in a suburb. His wife attended to customers during the day, while he went about his clerking, so that his income might, at least in part, be fixed. He sold to his fellow-clerks and practised on them an already persuasive tongue. He advertised with tact and adroitness, and now reaps the reward. He has done with clerking, and attends his shop himself with two assistants, and his wife is now given over to more domestic pursuits. In ten years from the date of his small beginning his photograph will appear in the trade organ, as a model and loadstar to young men in the business. Perhaps in another decade he will offer his business to the public.

At opposite poles from these types are the merchant princes, but they are less distinctive than the others, for their wealth, and perhaps,

The merchant princes also, their sons have worked great changes in them. They conform now to that type of successful man which is common to all commercial cities, and in so far they lose interest for us. Once

—Kew Terrace

on a lucky day when they were moneyless youths they found the horseshoe, which they sold for three halfpence to gain a start in life. Then they turned plain, unassuming men till fortune

came and honours blushed upon them, and they £10,000 a
suffered a sea change from the early simplicity. year
Their sons came home from English schools with
strange collars and stranger accents, to twist,
and reprove, and reform, and their daughters
married, perhaps into the army. Then arrived
the crowning honour of baronetcy and the
country seat, and a long adieu was bid to
the Glasgow man of old. But, after all, this
change to something higher would not seem to
have brought with it complete contentment.
Sometimes, you feel sure, the good man longs
for his early days when he lived in a circle with
conventions less foreign to his origin, with habits
more easy and perhaps more natural. You see
him in the street, and are rather sorry for him.
That look of care and oppression, and even
misery—whence has it sprung? Have his sins
come home to roost, or has the weight of all this
weary and unintelligible world settled, not on
his boyhood's, but on his manhood's shoulders?
No, it is merely this, that two hundred pounds a
year were " paradise enow."

Among the younger men, who have not yet
gained their character for life, you see many
types. The English public schoolboy is here,
as you always find him, fresh-coloured, clean-
looking, dressed with much skill and taste, and
every inch the nice boy of the ladies. It com-
forteth your soul to know (if you were bred at a
Board school) that he is often more for ornament

M

Kelvinside
versus
Pollokshields
than use, and that sometimes he is three-parts an ass. His chief merit is that he has made the home-grown youth an athlete and shown him the enormity of playing billiards in a tea-room in the day-time. Then you see the youth from the country, clumsy, and healthy, and ruddy, and without a trace of the precociousness or vice of a city-bred halflin. This man is often a lawyer's or architect's clerk, come from a country office to attend classes at the University or at the School of Art. He works with tremendous zeal, and will make a niche for himself in the city, and the county will have lost another good man. Again, you have the pure-bred Glasgow type which recognises the two varieties of Kelvinside and South Side youth. These are far asunder as the districts in which they live. They meet but never mingle, and continue through ignorance to regard each other with frank dislike. "Demn snob," says South Side, and Kelvinside retorts with "Poisonous bounder." Their interests in athletics differ. The Kelvinside is all for Rugby; South Side is divided between Rugby and Association. Also, they differ in their clothes. Kelvinside, with the English model living at its very door, is nearer perfection. South Side, it will tell you, is too curly in the brim of the hat, too daring in the cut of waistcoat, too tight in the trousers. An inch less all round and South Side, it will continue, had been the perfect gentleman. Once more, they differ in amuse-

ments.   South Side is the friend of bars and pantomimes and lighted streets; Kelvinside stays at home, or in each others' homes, dancing or billiard-playing and performing, in fact (as it will tell you), the ordinary social duties of civilised man.   And if after, say, an international football match Kelvinside should quit the West End for a night's adventure in the town, you notice another difference.   It goes not in single spies, but in battalions, which refuse to mix with outsiders, and know nothing of the fortuitous comradeship that is born in cups.   Yet, after all, these differences, serious as they are to the parties, are simplicity itself to explain.   The South Side is nearer the soil, the product perhaps of a cruder wealth.   Kelvinside is the South Side once removed.   A little while and the father of your same poisonous bounder will be your neighbour in a western terrace.   Yet a little while and his son may black-ball you at his club.

The man in the square hat has been described as the typical Glasgow man, because it is he that is seen most often in the business parts of the city.   But we do not forget that he is not the cause, but the product, of her greatness.   To a superficial eye he would seem to be a parasite buying and selling what other men produce, and yet he renders services to his fellows which justify his existence. Still it is not he who makes Glasgow a centre of industry and a home of manufactures.   That is a man of quite another kind, who is rarely seen on

"West is West"

The man who counts the streets, and, save to his own circle, is hardly known even by head-mark. He is to be found in the engine shops of Springburn or Govan, in the shipyards by the river, in the factories of the South Side and East End. We would gladly describe him, but we know him only by name. He controls a great enterprise of manufactures, and since that succeeds we assume that he has brains and inventive power, and a skill inherited or acquired. But what manner of man he is we cannot tell you. He does not live in the public eye, does not enter the Town Council (the haven under the hill for the square in hat), does not often rise to knighthood. The papers, indeed, mention his name from time to time, now as sitting as a man of skill on a Royal Commission, now as presenting pictures to the Corporation Galleries, now as being a leader in musical affairs, and always as a subscriber to the Lord Provost's charitable funds. And yet, for all the popular ignorance of him, he is the important man in Glasgow. For it is he and his kind that, by an ability far rarer and more specialised than the middleman's trick of selling and buying, keeps Glasgow in her place among the towns of industry. His are the original brains, which devise or adopt new ways to do old things, or invent processes to do old things and keep the industries vigorously alive. Glasgow depends on him for bread and butter, and this may be his recompense for obscurity. For, were the furnaces to be shut down, or the shipyards paid off, or the factories closed, destitution would march from Parkhead to Maryhill, and would teach the merchant that the producer is more necessary to a community than a middleman.

But the lesson is not, perhaps, needed, and if it were, it could be taught by a process less costly than famine. A little reflection will do, but if that be out of reach, and it is your part to drive the lesson home, remember that a few questions will shake to their foundations any false opinions of his importance to the city which daily contemplation of the Exchange may have bred in your merchant.

II

His Howffs

IT is not the accent of the people, nor the painted houses, nor yet the absence of Highland policemen that makes the Glasgow man in London feel that he is in a foreign town and far from home. It is a simpler matter. It is the lack of tea shops. You understand and sympathise with the question that he never fails to put to his southern friend, " A say, whit do you folk dae when ye want a good cuppa tea?" And the Londoner, what can he answer? Barring gin palaces and restaurants (where tea is equally tabooed) he knows no middle between, let us say, Fuller's on the one hand and a shop of the Aerated Bread Company on the other. Think of

Tea-rooms it ! Fuller's, the home of all that's expensive and
nice in cakes, the place so clean that every lady
lets trail her skirt ; and an A. B. C. shop, where the
very scones must be ordered like cuts from a joint,
and tea is set before one already mixed with milk,
as at a Sunday school treat.   Can elegance and
luxury reach a higher pitch, or shabby-genteel discomfort a lower depth?   What wonder if the
gangrel Scot from the Clyde returns with pleasure
to his town, where he may lunch on lighter fare
than steak and porter for the sum of fivepence amid
surroundings that remind him of a pleasant home.

Glasgow, in truth, is a very Tokio for tea rooms.
Nowhere can one have so much for so little, and
nowhere are such places more popular or frequented.   Edinburgh, it is true, has some pleasant
and charming rooms in haberdashers' shops, where
most dainty lunches are to be had for a trifle.   But
the Glasgow man has a delicacy in entering places
which ought, by rights, to be sacred to the other
sex ; and, if he does so, feels, perhaps, that he
might be better dressed.   In his own town he need
have no such qualms.   The tea rooms here are
meant for him, and it is he who uses them mainly.
They are independent enterprises, and they cater
for people with modest purses.   They are mainly
remarkable for two things—the scheme of their
decorations, and the location of some of their
premises.   It is believed (and averred) that in no
other town can you see in a place of refreshment
such ingenious and beautiful decorations in the

style of the new art as in Miss Cranston's shop in
Buchanan Street.   Indeed, so general in the city
is this belief that it has caused the Glasgow man of
the better sort to coin a new adjective denoting the
height of beauty; for in describing his impressions of some uncompleted buildings at the
Exhibition, he was overheard to use this climax:
" It is so kind o' artistic, ye know, wi' a' that sort
o' light paint. Oh, it'll do A 1 ! It's quite Kate

An Art Dealer's.

Cranston-ish !"   The other tea shops are less
ambitious, but all have come under the influence,
and the most fastidious man in the world
would find their colours agree with his eye.
Moreover, the arrangement of the tables is
pleasant.   These are not the bleak marble
things of the Edinburgh Café or an A. B. C.

The smoking room shop, but are made of wood, and are spread with fair white cloths, and set with flowers and china. The scones and cakes, too, are there at hand, to have and to hold. Nor is one overlooked while eating, lest, peradventure, fraud might occur. A printed notice certainly is sometimes there requesting the customer, in the interest of the management, accurately to remember the amount which he has consumed. But this is for the use of country cousins. In any case, the accounting is not otherwise controlled. One states the amount of one's indebtedness, and receives therefor a check from the attendant maiden. This, with the corresponding coin or coins, one hands in at the pay-desk, and so home. Nothing could be simpler or less irritating. *A bas les A. B. C.!*

The premises which many tea rooms occupy are remarkable also. Rents on good streets are high in Glasgow, but there is no lack of cellars, and if sufficient space cannot be had on the ground floor a cellar is generally to be found. And so places which before were given over to rats and lumber are now brilliant with electric light shining through tobacco smoke, for in the main it is the smoking rooms that are established below the pavement. They are wonderfully comfortable and well ventilated. A great part of their charm is to know one's self escaped from the traffic which rumbles dully overhead and disturbs not this place of quietness.

Of tea shops pure and simple there are now not

many in Glasgow. Stuart Cranston, who was the pioneer of the business, remains faithful to his first love, and in none of his shops in Buchanan Street and Renfield Street and Queen Street can you obtain anything more hunger-stilling than a sandwich. One or two other places follow his lead, but the rest are hybrids—part restaurant, part tea shop; but, of course, unlicensed. Sometimes (if space permits) there are separate departments for each kind of catering, but more often the distinction is maintained only in the furnishings of adjacent tables. Which is the more frequent customer, the tea-lunch man or the other, it would be hard to say. But even if it is the latter, the former has done a service in inducing the proprietor to make the prices for the dishes which he does not order, conformable to his purse. In the result you can lunch in Glasgow more cheaply, and with fewer additional imposts in the way of bread-money or tips than in any other town in Great Britain. For 1s. 4d. you can fill yourself drum-tight in an eating-house much more charmingly decorated than your home. If the tea-drinker has helped in bringing this state of matters about, it is but right that provision should be made for him in unexpected places. And thus in the Grosvenor Restaurant in Gordon Street, which is famous for its waiters and its 3s. table d'hôte dinner, and its band and its circular bars and its long-coated doorkeepers, you find an apartment where a retiring young man may have his " fivepenny wheck."

Tea room
customers

But the tea room, whether it be in a restaurant or elsewhere, is a popular place, and every kind of person comes at one time of the day or other. Our old friend, the plain, unassuming man, who now regrets the change of habits which bids him " tak his tea at denner-time, and his denner insteid o' his tea," he is there, and for his neighbour he may have the junior clerk of his rival in business. These people come between one and two, when the place is full of folks who lunch modestly, from necessity or caprice. But at four another kind of person comes—the lady who is shopping, or the smart youth who, two hours ago, had a most useful lunch at " Lang's," standing in the congregation of the upright. Others, again, come for the pleasures of the smoking room, which is the indispensable adjunct to a thriving tea shop. Here the clerk comes to his club, where his pals are sure to be found, and where everything that the heart desires, from coffee and cigarettes to illustrated papers and draughts and dominoes, is ready to his hand. Even an easy-chair, in which, after a night of dancing, he may be visited by sleep. No one, unless he is sitting on the *Sketch*, will wake him, for the place is Liberty Hall, and free to any one who has two-pence at disposal for a black coffee. This, indeed, is the only drawback, from the clerk's point of view, for his employer, on a voyage of discovery, must also hit upon the cosy howff, and sitting down beside him, engage him in conversation so

Saint Enoch Square
looking North.

embarrassing that his conscience is jogged, and he **"Miss!"**
departs, with some awkwardness, to his desk. But
be sure, our young gentleman will be there again
to-morrow, as regular as sunrise.

The girls who now are waitresses in tea shops
would have been domestic servants fifteen years
ago; to-day, they believe themselves better off,
in respect that they are called, not by their
Christian names, but by the vague title of "Miss,"
and that after a long day's work they have the
evening free for any occupation or amusement
that is compatible with physical fatigue. Their
wage is not large, and they lack the tips which
in a licensed restaurant will sometimes bring a
waitress' earnings up to five-and-thirty shillings
a week. Their food is provided, but the everlasting sight and smell of eatables makes the appetite
rather nice, and we fancy it is only the strong in
nerve among them who are hungry at meals. In
appearance they are often comely, and in
character above reproach. In one establishment
the aspirant, it is said, must produce a certificate
of character under the name of a minister of
the gospel; but in the others this is not insisted
on. It is more often a happy chance which
finds the girl employment. Once installed, she
may discover that a covey of young gentlemen
wait daily for her ministrations, and will even
have the loyalty to follow her should she change
her employer. This is the only point in which
she resembles a barmaid, from whom in all others

Tea shop as moral agent she must be carefully distinguished. She is less the Juno, and more the Cricket on the Hearth; less knowing, less familiar with the eccentricities of bibulous man, more quiet and domesticated. Then, again, she is generally Glasgow-born, and, to a student of idiom and accent, this is her chief merit, for (the accent of the barmaid being distorted by talk with English commercial travellers) she is the most accessible well of local English. To other people she has a more human interest, and to a young man coming without friends and introductions from the country, she may be a little tender. For it is not impossible that, his landlady apart, she is the only petticoated being with whom he can converse without shame. So the smile which greets him (even if given as readily to any other) is sweet to the lonely soul, and a friendly word from her seems a message from the blessed damosel.

It is said that the tea shops have done away with the daylight drinking which used to be common among Glasgow clerks a decade or two ago. Of these stirring times legends still exist in many offices, and the raw novice is told how, when the first of the month fell upon a Saturday, the whole staff, braving the " guvernors," would sally forth in the forenoon to a howff in Drury Street and leave the porter to keep the office; or how the process clerk of a lawyer's firm would each morning, punctually at ten, leave his desk under the pretext of " business at court," and late

in the afternoon return warm with liquor and less
than steady of foot. These days have gone for
good or bad, and the clerk of the period must,
at least by day, be reckoned among the sober
people. But he is quite as fond as his predecessor
was of going out on business. The smoking
rooms at any hour of the day bear witness to this.
And so perhaps there is something in the complaint of men who have come back from the hard
drinking of their youth, that tea shops are a
snare for the feet of the young. In the old days,
they say, to frequent a public-house demanded of
a man a certain inclination towards licence, a
certain disregard for propriety; in fact, a certain
pronouncedness of character. Hence youths of
rectitude passed by on the other side. Nowadays, the very innocence of the liquid purveyed
in a tea shop is the devil's own device for soothing
the conscience of the strictly bred. They enter,
thinking no evil, and at the end issue as tea-
sodden wretches that are worse than drunkards.
Moreover, they inhale the smoke of cheap
cigarettes.

If the tea shops are meant for the coming man,
clubs exist for the man who has arrived, and
public-houses for him who is overdue. But clubs
being what they are, one who is not a member
can speak only of their appearance and situation.
As to what passes within their walls, he has only
rumour for his source of information, and so his
opinion may be worth even less than it is taken

The Western Club for. But he may report without malice on their appearance from the street.

The only one which is a club, in the metropolitan sense of commanding from the lower

Saint Vincent Street

windows a view of a thronged thoroughfare, is the Western, which stands at the corner of St. Vincent Street and Buchanan Street (opposite, by the way, to the unofficial Press Club in Cairns' public-house). It is a very smart club, perhaps others the only one in Glasgow which is in any way exclusive. But the supply of clubmen of the right kind is not very great in Glasgow, and so this club rather lacks the white-haired, half-pay colonel, who might stand gossiping at its great windows and give to St. Vincent Street the air of a capital. The other clubs, excepting the Imperial Union, which is also in St. Vincent Street, but "one stair up," and the Junior Conservative, which occupies a dingy building in Renfield Street, with a wine merchant's shop on the ground floor, are in rather dull parts of dull streets. Even the Art Club, a place by rights of sweetness and light, is in Bath Street, which, as the home of doctors, is known, appropriately enough, as the Valley of the Shadow of Death. There, also, is the University Club, which is not more remote from the University than from the city. The Liberal Club, again, adjoins a hotel in an unfashionable part of Buchanan Street, but, on the other hand is opposite the Subway Station and near the Athenæum, a place of cheap culture. The Conservative Club is in Bothwell Street, and its very, very large building may have caught its look of a store for sanitary appliances from being situated opposite to a shop occupied by Messrs. Doulton & Co., Ltd. (of London, Paris, and Paisley). It is famous for lunches, this club, and on the days when the Tharsis Copper Company declares its dividend,

Spirit vaults there is served, they say, in a private room and
to shareholders only, a meal which would pervert
a vegetarian.   Otherwise, the building is convenient for both Central Station and Hengler's
Circus.   The New Club has a most imposing
house in West George Street, in a wilderness of
banks and offices.   It has rather the air of being
about to fall into the street, and for this reason,
perhaps, you never see any one at the front
windows.

There remain the public-houses for the overdue.
You cannot say that in Glasgow they have a distinctive character.   They are of the most ordinary
kind—brilliant, garish places, with barrels behind
the counter, sawdust on the floor, and the smell
of fermented liquor in the air.   They are purely
shops for perpendicular drinking, for the Magistrates, in the interests of the young, have
succeeded in making them places in which no man,
from the fatigue of standing, will linger long.
And this is the main reason why the "sing-
songs" and "cosies" which you hear of in
Manchester are unknown in Glasgow.   The
Magistrates will not grant a music licence to a
public-house.   But, perhaps, there is something
un-Scots in these random gatherings that would
make them distasteful to Northerns.   Smoking
concerts, though dreary past words, seem not to
be unpopular, when they are formally organised
and announced.   It is quite a different matter
to meet unbidden and unacquainted in some one's

public-house and spend a night of hilarity with **The poor man's club**
song and smoke and beer. It offends one's sense
of reserve, even one's self-respect, and perhaps it
is incompatible with the drinking of whisky.
That is the liquor which is, it seems, an end in
itself—the spirit, as it were, that purges the mind
of gross matters and passions, and leaves it aching
for dialectics, for argument, and conflict. Singing
may go with beer, but not with whisky. So the
public-houses of Glasgow are crowded, garish,
inhuman, unmerry places, to which men come for
refuge from the rain. They have no provision
for a continued sojourn. So rare are seats, that
if there chances to be a sitting-room in the shop
a ticket is placed in the window to announce the
fact. Thereby they encourage drinking, if not
in one particular public-house, at least in several.
For, after a while standing grows wearisome, and
the frozen stare of the barmen at your elbow
makes you unwelcome if you do not drink up and
have another, and so your idle person goes out in
the wet street, and once more, when the desolation
of the rainy night has seized upon him, enters
another public-house, to find as before that the
relief is short. Then out again, and in once more,
and so on till the clock strikes eleven, and the
devious direction is home. A natural instinct
for comradeship and brightness has driven him
from a squalid home into illuminated streets, and
from these the weather drives him for shelter to
the public-house. 'Tis his only refuge from

N

The ideal tavern   discomfort and weariness, and if he goes home drunk, he never meant to, and you cannot blame him.   The town makes no provision for giving to his day a gracious, sweetened hour, in which to blot out humanely and finely the memory of toil. This is the horrible side of humble life in Glasgow, and very soon it comes home to one that if that Something which, the wise agree, must be done to solve the Drink Problem, is ever to be accomplished, the beginning must be an improvement of the drinkers' houses.   And if that is a task too great for a municipality, or even for the State, then as a makeshift the publicans must be persuaded to change their shops into open as well as actual club-houses for the poor, in which not the only attraction shall be drinking.   The drawings might shrink, but the publican must bear in mind that he is a social pariah only because he is a social parasite, and that the loss to his purse might be the price of his advancement to esteem.   The wish is Utopian, of course, and the very hopelessness of realising it will give the advocate for municipal public-houses another argument for his cause.

III

Saturday

SATURDAY afternoon . . . it is the time of freedom, of leisure, of enjoyment.   The other days—from Monday to Friday—may be as grey and monotonous and uniform as if they were worsted stuff woven in the mills of God. They begin with labour and end with toil, and for, recreation only the night remains. But Saturday is a day apart. Half belongs to work and half to play, and in the latter half men shed conventions and reveal their natures.

Your clerk who goes to the country over Sunday, on this day appears in his office carrying a bag and golf clubs, and wearing his smartest and best. The very office is cheerful. The "guvernor" is away at golf. At best it is a half-day, in which work is no matter. It is good to stand before the fire and haver, or to engage in chamber gymnastics with desks for parallel bars and office seals for dumb-bells. And if a caller does appear, why, then, the glass screen about the counter fulfils its purpose. Chaff grows light-skirted, and jibes are flung and returned adroitly, and oh, it is very good to be alive. If only the creeping morning would wear quickly on to noon it were better still. Towards one o'clock unrest sets in, invincible. The gentlemen of the pen set about their preparations for departure. Office coats are changed for better; paper save-your-cuffs are detached and cast into the fire; hats are brushed and set with some jauntiness on straightened hair; the looking-glass goes round. The sun is out, and why on earth should we, that are fidging fain, be in? That clock with the laggard

One p.m. hands!—correct, precise and orderly, a very model of the man who must succeed. Will it never point to half-past one? Ah, there at long and last! Now mark my gentleman, his bag and golf-clubs lifted, slinking on tip-toe past doors that stand ajar and open on a sudden to disclose a partner that has no soul, calling him back to some task of urgency and importance. But a fig for employers! He has passed the swing-doors that are the gates to liberty, and is breathing a nimble air. Then down the street to the station that swarms with country-bound people, all eager to leave the city behind them. If he had time to see, he might notice a change in the character of the streets. Ladies are there, who set out a-shopping in the forenoon, and they, too, wear their smartest and best. Work-girls are there, hiving homewards in little groups, that laugh and chatter unendingly. Fathers of families are there, carrying in gloved hands the fibre baskets that contain fish for to-morrow's country dinner. Working men are there, eager to be home and " dichted," and ready for the " fitba' park " at three o'clock. The news-boys are out crying their wares and pocketing coppers. Everything, as the hour requires, goes like one o'clock. The throng at Renfield Street corner is great and jovial and gay, for work is over for a day and a half, and this is the best moment in the week. The cars pass up and down the hill, crowded within and without, and flying figures pursue them as if not another would pass

[180]

for a twelvemonth. It is Saturday afternoon, **The after-** you see, and time is very precious. A few hours **noon** and it will be Sunday, which was not made for pleasure.

As the afternoon wears on, you may, if you

Renfield Street

leave the frequented streets, see some curious sights. The business part of the city is now a deserted land. Caretakers that live in the basements of old dwelling-houses that now are offices,

[181]

On the river-side stretch carpets on the vacant pavements to air in the sun, or bring out pots of geraniums from their dwelling-rooms to set along area railings. Appearances, which till one o'clock were the life of the streets, now matter nothing. And a man might walk in shirt-sleeves and stockinged feet from one end to another unmolested. The air is full of peace, quietness, and sunshine, and the deadened sounds that float up the hill from busier parts sing in the ear to confirm the peace. Or you may go along the river-side above Glasgow Bridge, and see the gutter merchants who appear there on this afternoon only. One has a weighing machine, whose handsome seat upholstered in red plush is none too good for the men who live in Crown Street. Another offers Health Shocks for one penny, which are cheaper and more trustworthy than even patent medicines. Others, again, set up barrows of ancient, soiled, and faded books. Here persons come who care to loiter this afternoon of leisure, and browse on forgotten works. They are artizans of middle age, carpenters, coopers, and Radicals from their youth up, as Conservative as any Tory. Decent, quiet, grizzled men, with spectacles which they polish on green-black coats, before gloating over a new treasure. Sounds are muffled here, and disturb them not on their afternoon of secular rest. Before them is the smooth, dingy river, with poor men's clothing fluttering from the railing on its bank. A barge is moored in midstream, as idle as they are. On the other side are the roofs and irregular tenements of Gorbals, with **Dusk** steam blowing off from factory engines. Behind them is the Jail, and here under their fingers is literature at twopence. Strange stuff, too, that has here found a port after stormy seas. "The Mechanics' Guide to the Industries of Great Britain: London, 1843"—this he will buy because it is a book, and he is a mechanic. Or,

Gorbals Church from the Bridge

again, "A Gentleman's Tour through the States of Northern America" will be purchased, because, even to a Radical, the impressions of an aristocrat are precious.

As the afternoon wears on you find, if you return to the main thoroughfares, that the crowds have not withered away, but are changing character. Renfield Street and Sauchiehall Street are full of

"Fitba'" folk people passing homewards towards the west. Domestic couples go by, carrying little parcels for each other, and making pleasant pictures of contentment. Shop-girls, set free at four o'clock, are bent in the same direction. Matinees or afternoon concerts, "skailing" towards five o'clock, keep the westward-going throng thick and thicker. This is the hour when Renfield Street takes on its evening character. Quite suddenly you will hear a great clatter of wheels, and loud cries and shrill blasts of trumpets, and a brake full of men in "gravats" and "bunnets" rattles past you with a banner flying, and much clamour and loud chaff. These are the "fitba' supporters new back frae their gem." They are great strapping men, dight in their Sunday braws, and all belonging to the "Legion that never was 'listed." The business of their football club is other than to play, They "support"; they follow their team from field to field; they drive to and from the match in their brake; they wave their banner with the strange device—"Camlachie Shamrock 'Celtic' Football Club"; they roar obloquy and ridicule at any rival club whose brake may pass theirs. And they have solved, in a way, the problem of Happy Saturday Afternoons for the People. . . . Other supporters, who have slender purses or no club, follow on foot, and Renfield Street presently reeks of the game. At the corner the kerb is covered with men who stand with their backs to the light, intently reading in a pink news-

paper full of poetical reporting and results. Here
discussions begin that end in quod, and here
characteristic talk is heard.   This, for example—
" Haw Wull ! whit's the score ? . . . Hi man !
whit's the score ? . . . Whit the —— are ye
shouting at ? "   The repartee does not, indeed,
disclose the figures, but it reveals at least their
effect.

A little later you see the theatre-goers stream-
ing across Renfield Street corner.   The hour to-
night is a little earlier, and it is a very douce crowd

Waiting for the Evening Papers

you see thus bent on pleasure. A little later still
and Sauchiehall Street has become the street of
youth and the evening promenade. Here come
every night the young persons who have spent
the day cooped in shops or warehouses, or offices,
and who find sitting at home in dreary lodgings
an intolerable torture. On Saturday they come in
all the greater numbers—" the crood brings the
crood."   They have no other place in which to
spend spare time. The parks are closed after dark.
The Kelvingrove Park, which, it is true, remains

Sauchiehall
street—the
promenaders open, is given over to lovers, and is full of silence.
Theatres and concerts are too expensive.
The lighted street demands no admission money,
and so they come in droves. The girls, one hears,
come from the South Side—from Paisley Road—
because Paisley Road at night is a promenade for
dwellers in Govan. They go in couples, these
girls, in quiet enough dress—black jackets and
white sailor hats—and any minor differences are
repeated in each member of the couple. From
this you will infer that they are sisters, but
they are related only in the pantomime sense.
The men go also in couples, but more often
in crowds, and, as a rule, they are more repellent
than the girls. The real gent. is among them,
wearing the tan boots and signet ring which are
the differentiæ of his species. A long, light
brown coat, not looser than his mouth, a very low
waistcoat, suiting equally a jacket or a dress-coat,
a tall collar, and a bushy tie—these complete his
costume. He is rather loud and rather fatuous,
and does not know that in his button-hole he
wears " the white flower of the aimless life." As
a crowd you cannot call it gay. Bustle and stir
and life and brightness are there, but not laughter.
Now and again peal upon peal comes from a
little knot standing like an island in the traffic,
but it is hardly infectious laughter ; rather is it the
kind that is the protest against boredom, that
clutches at the smallest straw of merriment. A
knowing crowd, but only rarely vicious. On and on

[186]

in opposing streams they pace at a death's march. There is no reason for haste. When the one end of the street is reached they must turn again and seek the other. There is nothing else to do. Perhaps the maddening, slow pace, and the noise of the traffic fatigues them into silence, from which they can escape only by coming to a halt. Certainly, they are eager for diversion ; and so, when a juggler, or a street singer, an open-air speaker (socialist, evangelist, or atheist) occupies the poor man's platform at the foot of Wellington Street or West Campbell Street, he never wants for audience. Two of them may perhaps compete at the same time for the ear of the crowd, and then a great knot forms about them, and around it the opposing stream of passers-by swirl and eddy as round a sunken rock. The braw words rummle ower their heads, discordant, strenuous, and earnest, and they stand dumbly by, with never a sign of assent or dissent. It is a happy break, this, in an amusement grown monotonous, and so they stand and stand and listen ; and all the time a little, bent, old man is fiddling on a cracked fiddle a little jigging air that goes like an accompaniment to the idle, useless life on the pavement, which no one heeds. And over in another corner by the kerb one with the look of an ancient mariner invites the passers-by, in a gentle voice, for the price of one penny, to look through his slanted telescope at the mountains of the moon.

IV

The Working Man

The fitter HE is of the middle height, and strongly built,
and spare. His legs have not the robustness of
a countryman's, but are wiry, and suit well with
his body. His face has harsh features, which
give it character; his forehead has prominent
bones, his cheeks are fallen in, and the lines from
his nose to the mouth are strongly marked.
His eye is clear and bright, and his chin forceful.
His fingers, broad at the tips, and short, are those
of a clever workman. In dress he is not remarkable, but his bonnet and his blue turned-down
collar are characteristic. He lives in a tenement
in Govan, and his house consists of a room and
kitchen. He is married, and has four children,
and as likely as not his name is John Macmillan.
He was bred in the town, and before becoming
an apprentice in his works he was a message boy.
When his time was served he became a Union
man, and thought all the world of his District
Delegate. He is a very good workman, who
could turn his hand to many things, and make
a job o' them a'. He is intelligent, and has a
clear perception of injustice. But according to
his lights he is a reasonable man. He stauns up
for himsel' not only against the common enemy,
his employer, but also against his comrades in
allied trades if they invade his frontiers. He is

gruff, intractable, and independent, and his latent **His character and dialectics** irritability takes fire if his rights are infringed. Of servility he has not a trace. " Sir " is an unknown word to him, " Thank you " an unknown phrase. He is the perfect " Wha daur meddle wi' me." He has humour, but it is of a sardonic kind, for he has a keen sense of ridicule, and fears nothing so much as being made a butt. He has no mates, but goes with a crood. He is not sociable or aimlessly talkative, and an English workman would find it hard to engage him in conversation. He does not willingly tell of his breakfast or his appetite, or of his old 'ooman who attends to both, and if he is taken to task for his reserve, his answer will quite truly be, " Ay, man, but you fellies talk aboot things we widna be bothered talkin' aboot." He can be brilliantly indecent, and will argue on abstract points, and quibble with an indefatigable zeal. Among material themes he has a liking for fitba' and the gaffer, and on the latter subject he will break from taciturnity into cursing, perhaps as follows :—" He's a —— —— ——!" " Ay, an' he's a —— —— —— ——!" " That's jist whit he is, the ——!" Nor is he a domesticated man. His wife is too much with him in the room and kitchen house. And if he should spend the evening by the fire, most probably he will " take a read at the papers," and, when he is through with them, spend the hour till bedtime telling his wife of his own

His taste in drink

superiority as a workman to that —— that works alang wi' him. There are good reasons for his undomestic character, and they are connected, in the first instance, with his food and drink. He is not a great eater, for he cannot, like the Englishman, take four eggs to breakfast. Nor is he any hand at supper, which is as well, for since porridge went out of fashion, his wife is no cook. Then, again, his drink is not beer, which demands victuals as its accompaniment, but whisky, which requires none. And this drink, to be enjoyed, needs companions to be argued with, objects on which a purified mind may exercise a black-squad dialectic, and such persons are not to be found in a room and kitchen. His character and appearance are thereby influenced. For he is not plump and genial like the Englishman, but a spare, reserved, sardonic person, who, unlike the others, would not for his life be seen " demean himself " by blowing his weans' noses in a tram-way car. Of a piece with this is his unwillingness to be seen with his wife in public. She, " poor wretch," is mated to him for life, and why should they take the air together? He might very easily find her in the way. He could not, without offending a convention established among decent folk, take her into a public-house, and if he were to leave her outside he would hardly mend the matter. At a bar he might fall in with men he was " weel acquent wi," and might share in the round that was going; to withdraw then without

[190]

returning the favour were the part of a sponge. And to say his wife waited for him on the pavement were worse than no excuse. The finger of scorn would rise and the sardonic chaff, for which he and his kind are famous, would play about him. "A merrit man, God help 'um, a merrit man." And so his wife remains at home while he follows his own life. Partly the Magistrates are to blame. Their praiseworthy object has been to prevent the public-house from becoming what it is in England, the family sitting-room. They have made it an unlovely place, where the solitary person is not tempted to stay long after his liquor is over his throat. And women, except the poorest, do not frequent it. But the men by favouring the practice of "standing drinks round," have made it into their club, and so long as it is thus used, it works, together with overcrowded tenement houses, to make family life rather an impossible thing.

It is curious that our working man, who at ordinary times believes in "fair-do," and would regard a down fight in the Lancashire sense as something base and horrible, should lose his character when he makes one in the crowd at a football match, and that he will greet with a roar of delight some ungoverned brutality or clever, underhand trick, which, if practised on himself by a fellow-workman, he would resent until his dying day. The reason, no doubt, is that he has grown to take his pleasures fiercely, and that tricks of

Football and
morals

this kind are exciting if they escape detection.
His time for enjoyment is short, for his Saturday
has only twelve hours, and on the morrow descends
the pall of the " Sawbath " to smother pleasure.
His work, too, is hard, and now that he works
not with his hands, but in controlling a machine,
the demands on his attention have made his work
all the more exhausting. As his nights will not
serve for recreation, he must crowd into his
Saturday afternoon and evening the excitement
which shall compensate for a week of labour. So
football is his game, for no other can give the same
thrill, the same fierce exhilaration, the same outlet for the animal spirits which machinery has
suppressed. It is intoxication by the eye, and
to serve its purpose the game has become the
British bull-fight, and has made those who look
on at it as brutal and callous as any Spaniards.
Sportsmanship vanished alike from players and
spectators when the game became a trade, and
behind the referee's back everything is permitted.
If the offence is committed by his own side the
working man will not protest; •for it has given
him a new thrill. The players are his gods
until their powers decline, and for Jakie Robieson
or Big Jock wi' the Bunnet, it is roses, roses all
the way. Any man is proud to call them friend,
and talk is hushed when they take up the word.
And yet, if they are injured in the course of
their trade, they are considered merely as defective
parts of a machine, and are despatched to Matlock

for repairs. If the mending succeeds, good and *Quips of* well, but if not it is no matter, another part *argument* is on its way from the country, which is the maker.

The best you can say for football is that it has given the working man a subject for conversation. He turns it, at times, into an occasion for disputes, in which all the fierceness of the game is introduced, and so it is not unseemly that his friendliest discussions tremble on the verge of a bash on the mouth, and that his quips of argument are threats. But they are threats which lead to nothing, being intended for simple pleasantries which have their place when repartee for the moment fails him. " A'll pit ma finger in yer e'e " has an expressive gesture to accompany it, but no one takes offence. " Oot, ye swine ! " has less circumstance and leaves the threat to implication.

Yet he was not always a man of this kind. In his youth he showed promise of better things. He played his game himself in a park that was waste ground behind a tenement, and as bare of grass as the barren rocks of Aden. He had the ambition to become one day a player of note, but this suffered extinction when it came home to him that his friends' opinion of his " talent " was the right one. Then he left football for the concertina, and with other apprentices followed romance along deserted pavements, skliffing his feet to the tune of " Oh, Dem Golden

o

Halflin days Slippers," or breaking into that most pathetic of Glasgow sounds, an English music-hall song given with a local accent. He was not embittered in those days, or sardonic, or particularly thirsty for excitement, and if he had been taught how worthily to spend his leisure he might now have been a different man. But these excursions which led to nothing, even in the country, began to lose their charm, and perhaps he was to meet the experience of love, which taught him that one companion, with no concertina, was the right company for silent rambles along suburban roads. In due course, when his time was served, and he became a journeyman with a job, he married, and then, as he found that his condition but not his illusions were permanent, his character became what it is. His wife aye washing ; his own work the same, week in, week out, while that yisless—— that worked alang wi' him (no' a working man, but a maister's man) had every now and then a change of job, because he was weel in with the foreman. No wonder he took to the streets for his recreation, and joined the Kinning Park " Rangers " Club, and drove home in a brake from football matches with a melancholy company that found in barking cheers a relief from weariness.

Sunday gives leisure from labour and excitement, but is a day that he finds dreary and profitless beyond words. He spends his forenoon in bed, and, indeed, no one is stirring in his house until eleven, when his wife, in petticoat and

[194]

mantle, goes down to the dairy for milk. He His Sunday at
rises late and dichts himself with care, and then, home
in the *negligé* of shirt sleeves and stockinged
feet, he will spend the afternoon at his window,
watching the curious people who are more active
than himself. If his zeal for argument cannot
be curbed, he may wander to the Green, and hear

The Knife Grinder
& the Milkmen

for the unnumbered time the discussion on the
landlord's right to Poind yer Knock. But
with Picture Galleries and the People's Palace
closed, and music playing forbidden, he has
no means of worthily occupying his leisure.
When dusk comes, and he misses the week-day
brightness of the streets, he can but lounge against
a wall with companions as spiritless as himself.

The dull day The old discussions on the merits of football
players have lost their savour, now that whisky
is awanting wherewith to stir his mind and trim
it fair for argument.   It is not his fault.   No
provision is made for his amusement on the
Sabbath, and if it were, the day might become
too like Ne'er Day to be welcome.   That is the
nearest approximation to the Continental Sunday
which Glasgow knows, and if it did not swim in
and out on whisky it would be hardly more
tolerable than the usual one.   The shops are not
open, neither, by recommendation of the Magistrates, are the public-houses; but the trains run
and theatres are open.   There are eight football
matches, which are so arranged that an active
man may be present at two, but for all this the
day is dismal enough, and to make it a model for
the usual Sunday would be no great improvement.
We need a better climate to drive dulness out
of Glasgow; sunlight and blue sky to tempt men
to the country, or even to give a glory to
shabby streets.   Perhaps in time the parks
will have open-air restaurants and bands, and
the working man will have exchanged his gruffness
for something gayer.   At bottom he is a very
decent fellow, and his angularities may safely be
laid at the door of the conditions under which
he is forced to live.   He has in him much gracious
humanity, which kindly influences would bring
to flower.   It is only by way of reaction against
the dulness of a machine-made existence that he

[196]

takes to football and to drink. He is good to   **"Doon the**
his weans in a shamefaced way, but he is not   **watter"**
a demonstrative father, for he will usually intro-
duce wee Hughie and wee Maggie to a stranger
as this yin and yon yin. When he takes them
doon the watter on a Trades Holiday, he will lead
wee Hughie by the hand, while wee Maggie follows
with her mother forty paces in the rear, as if they
were the groom and he the young lady on horse-
back. When he reaches the "Benmore" his first
care is to settle his wife with the other women in
the bow, and as the voyage begins, his next is
to withdraw from society to examine the engines
with a friend, or, in the modern phrase, to shoot
auld De Wet with a pocket pistol. He reappears
when the boat reaches Lochgoilhead, and the
passengers are invited to spend on shore the
thirty minutes which the time-tables advertise.
Then he will play gaffer to his wife, collecting
packages and her umbrellas, and will bid her (to
see that all's well) coont the weans. But these
single holidays are trying to the temper, and
he finds the Fair Holidays, with its fourteen days
of a rainy July, more to his mind. In recent
years he has taken to spending it at Coleraine
and Portrush, where he revives on another shore
his halflin's romance of sleeping out in Skeoch
Wood. Not so long ago he was content with
Dunoon, where he could set out with another
man in a sma'-boat, while his wife sat on a rock
on the shore and cried on wee Hughie to come

"Doon the watter"

back oot o' that this meenit, or her word, but she would wairm his lugs when she catched him. It is perhaps a pity that he now goes to Ireland, for he has taken his dialect with him, and now Irish ears hear what used to be a Glasgow man's

Corner of High Street
and George Street

delight, the cries of trippers escaping from danger of collision with river steamers. "Pu', paw, pu'; oh, my paw, can ye no' pu', paw?" has, it is believed, been heard at Dunoon for the last time.

[198]

East End —
"Six o' clock"

There is another type of working man, whose **The radical Calvinist** way of life differs from that of the first, although his character is in essentials the same. This is one of an older type who seems to have adapted himself more perfectly to the conditions of his existence, and to have acquiesced without protest. He does not need the excitement for which the other craves, and so he does not care for football or whisky. His interest in argument is not less keen, but his discussions are political or theological. He is a radical and Calvinist by inheritance and tradition, and though his active interest in Calvinism may have abated, its principles still control his conduct. He was not born for gaiety or keen pleasure, and the greyness of his work and his town does not oppress him. He is the pink of respectability, from his parlour in Crown Street to his Sunday blacks. He finds his occupations at home, in making model yachts for his grandchildren, or in reading the *Weekly Mail*, and he and the wife get on fine, with few words. He is the backbone of the working classes, but though he is above the ruck he does not, unfortunately, change its character.

V

Quayside Folk

Quay life in
the city

THE sheds which line the river from Glasgow
Bridge to Finnieston contain a life of their own,
none the less curious because no one has anything
to say about it. Those who could tell its stories
are occupied with more fashionable business
and come not near, and the inhabitants see nothing
odd in themselves and their environs, as is indeed
the manner of all inhabitants from Whitechapel
to the Pitcairn Islands. But sometimes the quay
intrudes its affairs into the city. One day you
may find your car stopped at the foot of Jamaica
Street, while a drove of huge Galway cattle
thunders along the Broomielaw, seeming beside
the electric wires and monumental policeman
almost as foreign to the eye as a herd of zebras.
And behind them dance as strange a group of
two-legged figures—a couple of yelling Irishmen,
ragged and wild-eyed, and shouting in their rear
an army of gosoons, each with his stick that is
taller than himself. At another time your
attention may be attracted by a quaking but
optimistic crew of Lascars, doing their best to vend
gilded sea-shells and peacock feathers to the Argyle
Street scoffer ; or by a noisy seaman defying that
section of the public which calls themselves men
to take off their coats—damn them—just for five
minutes ! But in the main the quay life is not

visible beyond its borders.   Yet it is here that The emi-grants
the seasons which pass so unnoticed in the town
arrive, each with its appropriate tableau.

In spring there are the emigrants making for
the American boats—Polish Jews, Finlanders,
Germans, and Czechs, marching stolidly beside
their hardy, clean-eyed women-folk, speaking not

Custom House Quay

at all, looking neither left nor right ; pilgrims on
their way to a promised land.   With summer
comes the great Fair exodus, when the native
boards his " doon the watter " boat at Broomielaw, and the poor Irishman returns to his own
land to show the ould folk his grand new watch,
and to negotiate for the sack of potatoes that

The quay calendar is to be his winter's rations. And when the swallows are flying south, the Irish harvesters, who come over in small parties all through the summer, return in a multitude, crowding all the boats on the north quays. The sun-browned harvester, one of the few picturesque types left to us in modern days, cuts a fine figure in his light homespun clothes and parti-coloured kerchief, as he straggles from tavern to ship and ship to tavern in merry bawling parties, for work is over for the year, and there will be a warm fire-cheek in his cabin this winter. When they are gathered inside the sheds, the mild grey light of the quays displays a spectrum of reds and blues and yellows and violets that make it the gayest spot in Glasgow. But this pageant of colour seems dull when their countrywomen arrive a month later—the stout little Irishwomen who gather the Scots potato harvest every year, and are now on their way home, with a five-pound note in their stays to fend off the hard winter on the barren coast villages of County Mayo. These high-complexioned, red-haired women speak a tongue more strange than French to Glasgow ears, and in their bright shawls and skirts, their immense brown hobnailed boots, they seem as alien as the Czechs themselves. The signs of winter are more varied. There is the arrival of holly and fowls and mistletoe and stuffs for the Christmas market; the rush in the cattle trade; and the coming and going of the theatrical

[202]

company (the hero as sea-sick as the villain), and the awful days of fog on the river, when no man may call his horse and cart his own.

But apart from the strangers that pass and repass in their appointed season, the everyday life of the quays presents as racy and varied a field of character as ever met the unheeding eyes of the novelist. Up in the city, whither the shipping clerk goes after a proper brushing of his hat, you can only tell a man by his tie or the cut of his beard; but in his little wooden castle the clerk knows his friends in other ways. Here men speak as if their voices were their own. The Irishman who came over and began the business of "commission agent" as soon as his father had a dozen good-laying hens has still, for all his twenty years in Stockwell Street—or perhaps because of them—his full, rasping Ballymena brogue; and the skipper in cross-channel service, labour over, converses, if not in Gaelic, at least in the clean, pleasant tongue of the Highlanders— English shorn of idiom. The clerks, the checkers, and the labourers are from the country nearly to a man, and keep their health and accent uncontaminated by Glasgow's smoke and Glasgow's unconsonantal drawl. To be in one of the checkers' boxes of an evening, when the stages are drawn and the trucks are piled at the end of the shed, is to be in a very good place. Checkers are made, not born, and the men have always seen many trades—even shepherding on

The
"checkers"

the Galloway hills, or acting the master of ceremonies to East End " jiggers "—before they settled down to this one. They are rolling stones, and as like as not may to-morrow be roaring the odds on a racecourse or on their way to South

The Suspension Bridge .

Africa. Not that they are unsatisfied with things. See the checkers looking across their quiet street when the works are skailing, and the bent, grimy squadrons hurry past. They look on with something of pity in their glance, and

204]

GLASGOW OF FICTION

one will say : " But, man, they've nae head-work, **Quay Parliaments** like coontin' empty egg boxes." You are listening to a man, restless, certainly, but not at odds with destiny. He is good company, the checker, and at home on all subjects, from co-operative dividends to the doings of the fairies in Skye, and these he will discuss in the light of personal experience. The little quay parliaments, which sit in those wooden houses on wheels along the river, are constituted by the checker and his friend the railway foreman, the carter, the small commission agent, the old men far down in the world who push their fortunes in wool-brokers' wheelbarrows, with perhaps a policeman or two, and inevitably the queer gaberlunzie men who live in this region and no other. There they lounge out the last half-hour to the stroke of six, or on foggy days await the boats that lie somewhere in the river. The place is thick with smoke, and in the winter nights a great debate is carried on in the light of the fire. Sometimes the flames leaping up as the men bend forward in excited argument, carve for a moment out of the darkness the gaunt head of a Covenanter, or the wild reincarnation of some Highland fighter; then the crowd are in shadow again, and you are listening to the voices of lang Wullie Johnstone and old Jamie Mathieson, the quay messenger.

If one has a mind for the little pleasures of observation, and is not cursed with a delicate nose, one might do worse than be a shipping clerk in

[205]

the Glasgow quayside. The clerk pops out and in his box all day long, just as do the pigeons in their dovecot over his head. Your proper head clerk is a kind of bonnet laird, who lives among his dogs and hens and turkeys, with maybe an old horse at the far end of the shed, and a sheep which—provided it is not demoralised by the lumpers into eating tobacco—is an ornament to any shipping business. The place is always like a farm, with piles of golden hay in the sides and grain on its floor. It is never free of cattle, and the head clerk holds long converse with dealers over the season's prospects and the North-Country fairs. In his office a handful of new laid eggs lie among his papers, and he will stop in the middle of his cash entries to run into the shed at the sound of an unprofitable hen clucking confidently at last. The under clerk is not like your office man, who has a guv'nor unsoothed by Arcadian joys, and no one but a boy to command. There are a company of checkers who say to him, " A'll see to it that it's dune, richt enough, when so be " ; or a legion of lumpers who cry at the proper time, " Beggin' your pardon, sir, ye've drapt your pen." He acquires a curious, left-handed kind of knowledge from the broken men who now work the cargo, and the Highland mariners, which will not, perhaps, advance him towards a cashier's job, but makes him a good deal more interesting to his fellow-creatures. He learns many strange things, for the quayside is the harbour of wandering dogs and lost men. The dogs find their way there, I have been told, because they strike the river in their wanderings, and as they can go no further, prowl about and sleep in the sheds until the cattle " pelters " find them and put them to learn the trade of driving cattle, or return them to their owners and earn reward. But no one knows why the lost men come here— the Welsh master of foxhounds, who now follows his truck with as much abandon as he did his own hounds ; the disrated captains of Atlantic steamers ; the inventor, who can devise nothing to cure his own curse ; the Irish squireen, who runs errands for men as seedy as himself ; the San Francisco editor, who writes " penny horribles " in a little tobacco shop, and would have been famous for ever with his " International League of Mechanics and Labourers of Britain and America," but for the spies who haunt his lodgings (he will tell you) day and night ; the man who does odd jobs along the quay—a national hero, this, when he returned with Hobson after they had sunk the " Merrimac " in Santiago—and all the curious derelicts that call the harbour home. Perhaps they come down to the quayside to set out to their lands of promise, or have arrived on the return voyage. Or it may be that many desire to be near ships should the police ever come bothering about some " small affair " of the past ; or more likely it is because

Lost dogs and queer fellows

Quayside legatee the quayside is a state by itself as homely and incurious as Alsatia, where eccentricities will be tolerated, and even observed with pleasure. It is a place, too, where men turn philosophers, and where money is less considered than in the city mart.

One such philosopher was John Smith, a quay labourer, but a man of family and some time a

man of substance in Wales. To him fell a legacy of a thousand pounds one day, and his way of spending it could only have found proper sympathy at the quay. It was most simple. He placed his wife and three children inside one of the old quayside growlers, and the legatee sat himself on the box beside the driver. At every tavern they stopped and the driver brought out

drinks. Smith drank on the box, his wife A marine
in the cab, and the driver on the street. And so philosopher
to the next one. Then home in the evening,
hallooing along the quayside to the delight of the
neighbourhood. He did not forget past days, but
lent money lavishly and filled the lumpers so
"fou" that a boat missed the tide and the whole
shed was demoralised for weeks. A short life, but
a merry one, my masters. First the old horse,
sickened with perplexity as to when the fare would
end, dropped off after ten weeks of it. Then, and
just before the old driver was about to follow—
reluctant as he was now that life had at last
blossomed to him—the thousand pounds ran out,
the last twenty going to pay for a chemist shop
which Mr. Smith wrecked to express disapproval
of the doctor's not wearing his tall hat when he
called on his wife.

A week later John Smith, Esquire, became
"Jake" once more, bending his broad back in the
trucks without a single show of regret. And his
wife, although she misses her outings, seems not
unreconciled to her lot so long as her husband
can sport of a Sunday his Newmarket coat and
blue waistcoat as outward and visible signs that
they were carriage folk in their day.

Smith was a philosopher, I am inclined to think,
and his wild months are to be read as a proper
scorn of adventitious wealth; but when you come
to consider Alexander Garden you touch a pro-
founder depth, for Alexander was a man who not

P

His plans of livelihood only scorned riches, but saw clearly the absurdity of human labour in this most haphazard of worlds. He was of some moment in the neighbourhood, and had spent thirty years of his honest life stepping in and out of the sheds preaching his gospel of good-fellowship; as often drunk as sober, but more often in a state which combined the virtues of both. True, he humoured the world by keeping up a pretence of working, for Alec was, as he would tell you, " a dailing man, no less." He dealt sometimes in matches, sometimes in shoe-laces, and once in oranges, but his stock-in-trade could at all times be stowed away in one pocket when danger threatened. What money Alec made—for a man, after all, must live—was earned by standing at the entrance to one of the Irish sheds directing the passengers to the boat which lay in plain sight. His method was to awe his countryman with a wave of his walking-stick, give him a short account of his life and character—" Twinty years in the Darry sheds and never stole an egg in me life, young fellow, me lad; an' they'll tell ye that at the affice." Alec would lead the passenger to the office, where the clerks would confirm his story, then he would point out the Darry boat, apply for a copper for a " cup o' caffee," and, if it pleased Providence, get tipsy with his new acquaintance. How he managed to live and keep a smile on his queer old face these twenty years passes understanding. When passengers were few or wary, Alec had business transactions with the clerks and checkers, which left the clerks with a very inferior box of matches and Alec with twopence. He would also keep the flies off the splendid plum-puddings in the Broomielaw cookshop windows, or hold a very tame dog for a consideration. On fair nights he slept in empty egg crates (and once was trucked into the steamer and almost stowed away in the hold); and in bad weather he got shelter some-where, knowing all kinds of lee corners, like the old campaigner he was. Still, upon my soul, no one could call the man unhappy. Through many a dirtier trick than ever Falstaff suffered, the eternal good humour of the creature never deserted him. The younger lumpers held that he was daft, and in order to make this more clear tied old greasy sacks round his bald head, stole his hat and coat, and baptised him in water of Clyde. But Alec forgave the lads and bore them no malice. He had a bad word for no man. " Red Mick," the cattleman, who had done his mate to death by the knife, and " Scrunt," the loadener, whose proud boast it was that he had bitten half the Marine Division of the police force, were his associates—though never his friends. He held open views on the morality of others ; but he had his own code of honour. Beyond saying " caffee " when he meant whisky, he told no lies ; had a proper pride of his own (there were men in office that Alec would never ask for " a cup o' caffee although he had been starving for

His appearance

years "). Civil spoken to every one, interested in
his curious, childlike way in all things, from railway
disasters to other people's funny way of speaking,
and full of sympathy to " ould fellas " or men he
considered mentally deficient, such as policemen,
Alec lived the open-air existence that he loved. A
little, stoutish fellow he was, with a round, bald
head, and a nose cut by a fall on some lodging-
house stair. I think the oddest thing about the
starving old gaberlunzie was his habit of shaving
clean whenever he had the money. If he preserved any vanity from the old days when he had
a wife, was a stage-end man, which is a corporal of
lumpers, and wore every Monday the most spotless
moleskins ever seen on the quay, it ran to nothing
else, for his clothes were like those of a scarecrow,
although he wore them with some style, and his
hands were never clean. Once the curious put it
to him why he shaved? " Just a way o' doin',"
said Alec Garden.

Alec had a brother who lived twenty miles
beyond some Bally, and this brother was a
wealthy man, " with a farm o' land and a carn
mill." Every spring when the weather was fine,
and the old grandfathers who sit by the fire in
dark kitchens of Anderston begin to totter out into
the sun and sit on the empty barrels at the shed-
mouth, Alec would go round telling his friends
that he was off to Bally-something where his
brother had the farm o' land and the carn mill.
He would collect waterproofs and sticks and small

tin boxes, and the like, but autumn came with Outward
Alec Garden still in the sheds. Twice, it is true, bound
he did go, but each time returned in a week or so.
" His brother put ould Alec to cuttin' the carn,"
his enemies said, but Alec himself would tell you
that he " cud not allways be stopping over there,
d'ye see."

As time went on the " caff and a spit," which
was Alec's one complaint against the gods that be,
never left him. One day, for the first time in
his life, Alexander Garden was driven away in a
carriage, and the old cherubic face, like the grey
battered visage of some wooden cupid on a
ship's figurehead, passed out of the life of the
quay. A useless old philosopher, perhaps, yet
the place was the emptier, and it seemed as though
the little wooden admirals in Clyde Place had
dropped from their perch, or the old crusted
time-ball on the Sailor's Home had fallen.

VI

Suburbs by the Sea

The quiet life WHEN the Glasgow man is at a popular English watering-place he finds himself in a foreign and unreasonable land. At home he lives in a flat, with strange neighbours on every side of him, and the privacy of his life is distinctly under protest. On holiday he seeks to live a simpler life, where he may find the quiet pleasures the town denied to him—a garden, a boat, and the wearing of his old clothes. He would have a cottage with trees, roses at its porch, a lawn where after dinner he may sit within his gates and bring an ancestral telescope to bear upon the steamers and the yachts; his boat at its specific buoy, where he may haul it in at any hour his fancy dictates—at morning when he and his lads go off to bathe, or at evening when the inevitable rain has left the loch streaked and glazed as a skating pond, the hills are shaking off their mists, and he lights his pipe as he crunches over the sea-weed to go a-fishing.

[214]

The many-mansioned tenement, with its Coast days modern conveniences, the pavements, and the gas lamps, the strange folk who rub shoulders with him on the stair are behind him and forgotten. He and his wife are at peace with Nature. Even though he be a bailie, his boys may go barefoot, and he himself, provided his silk hat is prepared against the Sunday, may lounge away the quiet evenings with a pipe in his mouth. And should something in the air of Saturday night, with the water near the pier trembling at the unwonted light in the village shops, and the bagpipes sounding somewhere in the dark, give his thoughts a sentimental turn, he may appear to his wife in the suit of clothes he proposed in, and even dance on the green without being thought the less well-dressed and respectable. His holidays pass simply and pleasantly, with perhaps a shade of dulness. He is moved by the new sense of cleanliness in the air, and away from the garish streets, he rediscovers night. He snuffs candles and goes to bed early, revives his interest in flowers and birds' nests, and makes acquaintance with his children. Having gone to Glennaquoich year after year, he knows his neighbours as his sons know the steamboats, and joins them at the village inn over a glass of toddy when the nights grow cold, and together they support the local sports and boat races. The fishermen he knows, as far as a city man may know a Highlander; the piermaster

Sentimental will teach him the meteorological signs to be
observed on the hills "chust close by"; the
policeman will admire his collie and his tobacco,
and he will find himself altogether a man of
some weight and countenance. If he is very
lucky, too, solid years of business may slip from
him in those peaceful Herrick-like days, and his
boyhood and courtship may peep at him over the
hedge. Sometimes poetry—though possibly he
may not call it so—touches him to consciousness.
Fishing with line at evening at some secret spot
away past the point, where, as every villager
knows, you anchor mid-way between a sheep-
fank on the bare hillside and a clearing in the
firwood, while the hills grow greyer and greyer
as the twilight fades out of the waters, the city
man feels within himself something of the ancient
patriarchal emotion as he and his sons are alone
in their four-oarer, on the floor of the dim loch,
with the stars overhead, and the phosphorescence
lapping round the boat. No sound on the hills
or the sea, save when a heron rises sudden from
the reeds on the shore, or when a dark fin cuts
the blackness into diamonds, and a porpoise turns
over near the boat and tells you that your fishing
is done for the night. Then the long row home
round the bends, with only the sound of dripping
oars breaking the stillness, till the cottage with its
lit windows and white walls shines like a lighthouse out of the darkness, and his girls come
down to the jetty to coo-ee a welcome, and his

boys make answer boasting of their take.
The scattered lights at the margin of the
loch beneath the silent hills, and sound of young
voices in the great Highland twilight seem to him
to hold, as in the past, whatever of poetry and
of the beauty of life has entered into his scheme
of things.

This is the coast life of the city man of
moderate means and large family, of the plain,
unassuming man who, if he has not arrived in the
harbour of wealth, has put into a good port.

Our vignette, it will be said, is not typical;
Glennaquoich, with its solitary policeman, its
village inn, its old clothes, and rare neighbours
cannot be found in Rothesay, or Dunoon, or
Largs. Its life is quite foreign to these times,
when the English Bellevue-by-the-Sea sets the
fashion for the Clyde resort, and, indeed, one must
admit that it is not Glennaquoich which first
takes the eye of the tourist. He may explore its
fjord, and be charmed by the simple and lonely
beauty of the life that it reveals, but he does not
know that the Firth and the Lochs hold a hundred
spots as fair. But he may take it from me that
the Glasgow man is far prouder of these hundred
nooks than of his Madeiras of Scotland and
Brightons of the North.

A firth of Glennaquoichs is an impossible ideal
as the suburb of a great manufacturing city, and,
indeed, the only wonder is that it exists as the

[217]

Rothesay and
Dunoon

ideal of any portion of the inhabitants, and that Rothesay and Dunoon, places so inevitably the ideal for the overworked clerk and anæmic shopgirl, are on the whole so tolerable and unspoilt as they are. The bay and the view give to Rothesay a character and charm which even legions of trippers cannot alter. Across the water you see the Argyllshire Highlands rising as lonely and untrodden as any peak in Darien, and in the town itself you will find, facing a cluster of tenements, an ancient castle that rises behind its moat and trees, beautiful and grave and romantic despite its mean surroundings. The visitors who come here are of all classes. In mid-July the Glasgow artisan with his family "stops" here for a fortnight; the business man—our Glennaquoich man who, for reasons of state, has no choice—"stays" here in August; and English tourists on their way to the North "live" at the Hydropathic for a day or two in September.

Dunoon offers you a walk by the sea with the beautiful Firth at your side, somewhat tarnished, it is true, by steamer smoke. At one time the town may have been known as Argyle-Street-by-the-Sea, but Sauchiehall Street has changed all that, and the shore, where "feyther gethered the dulse and wee Hughie's tae had the adventure with the partan," is now unfrequented, for your blade and his lady wear here their best clothes, and these must last ten crowded days. There is an excellent cycling road (that leads round Holy Loch **Renfrewshire coast** and up Loch Long, till it loses itself suddenly, just before the Carrick Castle folk can make your acquaintance), a perfect navy of small boats, and a "Castle Garden" that is not unbeautiful, and can be best enjoyed from a boat in the bay at night when the lamps are lit and the band is not over-near.

These two towns are Glasgow's greater suburbs by the sea, but—putting aside Kilcreggan and Blairmore, and other places that are merely Glennaquoich's clachan grown big—there are many others of importance and character. As a rule, the visitor to the Clyde first makes its acquaintance at Gourock, where the Caledonian Railway's yellow-funnelled steamers begin their journeys. This spot was famous once for its view and its bay. A certain popularity is still left to the bay as a winter refuge for yachts, but the view has nowadays rather lost its name, because travellers in their haste to be off and on the steamer will not look at it. Yet nowhere is the sunset scene more stately and West Highland, and to no place do the hills above Loch Lomond present a grander outline. Once out in the Firth you find yourself on a sunny day in a most enlivening and happy scene. As far as the eye can reach, the little villas twinkle along the shore at the bottom of the hills, and the blue sea is inlaid with the white sails of yachts. The Ren-

frewshire side is steep and wooded, but rises to
no great height. A road runs along the water's
edge as level and as straight as a die, and on the
heights above it are red stone villas that belong
to the funded wealth of Glasgow. Stately, dull
homes these, too near one another for perfect
privacy, and too distant for company. In front
of some of the goodliest a steam yacht is at anchor
—a carriage waiting day and night, which affronts
the plebeian. The town of Largs, which is
Paisley-super-Mare, winds up the long parade of
riches with a sudden and sturdy contrast, which,
however, is somewhat superficial, since the two
great red churches—each big enough to hold her
whole population—are the gifts of millionaires of
her hinterland. Lower down is Fairlie, with the
yacht-building yard from which a dynasty of Fifes
have launched some of the most famous racing
yachts in the world. Still lower down the Firth
is the Land of Golf (with Barassie, Gailes, Troon,
and Prestwick) and the Land of Burns. If you
are a Common Burnsite you will find in (or near)
Ayr the Cottage and the Monument to give you
inspiration against the next " Nicht o' Nichts,"
and routh of taverns for drowning criticism. Over
the Firth Arran starts out of the sea ; and Arran,
Ayr, and Burns are connected in this way, that
Burns lived at Ayr and never wrote a word about
Arran. And yet the Island has outlines which the
sunset clouds themselves repeat as past excelling,
and it looms out of the mist in cold, pale days

as shadowy a haven for passing ships as any in the Arran sky above it. When night falls it is the enchanted island of a boy's dream, and Goatfell and his mysterious volcanic brethren are the Mountains of the Moon. And Burns saw all this from his Auld Brig, where the view is best, and said never a word.

If you visit the Island you will find it the Highlands in essence and miniature, a land with a king of its own, in which neither game-keepers nor deer seem out of place, a land of mountains and desperate glens, and roads that

Arran from across Bute

lead to nowhere. The tiniest fringe of it is inhabited, and in the company of such hills and of such black nights the city man forgets his pavements, and becomes a part of Nature. The people are unspoiled, being some fifty years behind the times. A dozen years ago, they say, an Arran man (a sergeant of police) stole out in the night-time and buried below low water-mark the boots of a murdered man, to protect the Island from the evil chance. They have the Gaelic, and keep the Sabbath after the old style, and they are a lazy, kindly, primitive folk, with ways that will not be altered, as the visitor finds

The Isles if he desires to breakfast before leaving by the early boat on a Monday morning. It is they and not townspeople who own the houses on the Island. In the summer they give up their dwellings to visitors, and the hens in turn render a like service to them.

Near Arran are the adjacent Islands of Bute, Cumbrae, and Great Britain—all of much less interest. Bute possesses, besides the town of Rothesay, the domain of its noble marquis and a well-cultivated interior ; and Cumbrae, the bright

little township of Millport, on whose yellow sands and trim " Garrison " the sun shines happier (they say) than anywhere else. Great Britain, for the purpose of these notes, may be considered to mean Helensburgh, Tighnabruaich, Colintraive, and Tarbert, besides the places already touched on. Helensburgh lies at the mouth of the pretty, midge-ridden Gareloch, known to the Glasgow man either as a place of mild air in spring, as a house of call for cyclists, or as the starting-point of the North British paddle steamers. Tighnabruaich and Colintraive are in the Kyles of Bute,

a narrow strip of sea that winds between Bute and The Kyles
the Mainland, no wider at parts than the steamer's
beam, beautiful enough to fill a photographer
with the grace of God, and so splendid that poet
and painter have left it to speak for itself.
Tighnabruaich is less Highland than its name. It
is a little cluster of villas, that might be Innellan's,
sitting among trees on the water's edge, with a
great bare hill behind it. But to my fancy its
cheery little face in this remote spot—more
remote, it is true, in impression than in reality—
always has a look of anxiety, as if it cowered
through the winter on this precarious shelter,
while the storms that rush up the deep channel
between Arran and Kintyre were thundering on
the rocks of Ardlamont. The sun plays strange
tricks in this region, where the hills make their
own arrangements of light and shade, and the
little inhabited places that lie in steep glens take
on curious shadows, and are visited by something
other than the light of common day. In the valley
of the Kyles is Colintraive, nothing more than a
little jetty and an inn, with a road that comes
tumbling down the hill behind it like a burn;
and here the loneliness is deeper. Men come to
the place in gigs, and after the steamer has called
depart again to the country behind the hill. You
understand when you see them at the pier the
reverence in which they hold MacBrayne's red
funnels.

Tarbert   Round Ardlamont Point, Loch Fyne spreads
itself away to the north-west, cold and glittering
as its own herring. On both sides low, craggy hills,
with sometimes a burr of trees and a shooting
lodge, stretch a blue unending line along the sky,
and on the side where the watery twilight lingers
till nigh morning, there is a creek which two
steamers every day discover, and in it the fishing
village of Tarbert lies hid. Tarbert, it is true, is
not a suburb by the sea, and hardly comes under
the scope of these notes, but I include it here
because it seems to me the kind of place that
the others were before Glasgow made them
suburbs. It has traditions, associations, and a
character of its own; the natives have not yet
realised that politeness, which costs little, has a
money value. They are a prosperous, bien people,
owning fishing smacks and weel-biggit stone
houses. They mind their own business at the
proper season, and at other times drink whisky,
often having their "morning" with a Royal
Academician (by Gad!), and the echoes of their
stories are heard on Show Sunday. Dressed
in their jerseys and fine blue cloth waistcoats and
trousers, they present to the visitors one long row
of immobile backs as they sit at the harbour-end
with their feet dangling over the quay.

The place itself is an irregular congregation of
houses, each seemingly bent on scrambling further
up the hillside than its neighbour. It is situated
at the head of a twisting creek that is shut in from

[224]

view of the loch by high hills. As it suddenly Yachting
discloses itself round the bend, with its suspicious
little island in front, and the fortress look of its
buildings, it has always seemed to me—despite the
respectable gait and look of the inhabitants—to
have the appearance of a Pirate's Lair. The
village has a life of its own, untouched by
visitors' clubs, and the stranger from Glasgow is
a person of next to no importance. In the 'fifties,
when Govan was "doon the watter," the Firth
must have been studded with such places as
Tarbert, only less romantic in aspect and less
prosperous in reality. Now it is rare to come on
so unspoiled a township, and it is good once in a
while for the wee Glasgow man to stand the cold
contempt of those broad, blue backs.

Our Glennaquoich friend and his betters—
better, at a guess, by ten thousand a year—the
decent city youth, and even the blade have a
common interest in yachting. It is the only sport
that all classes follow seriously. Football has the
favour of the mob; Rugby football is a West-End
interest; the horse-racing at Hamilton is maintained by sporting publicans and their customers;
but yachting has the favour of every class. The
workman who "kent a man that wrocht on the
'Britannia' at Hennerson's," and the city man
whose only wager in a blameless life was a silk
hat against a square one on the result of the
America Cup, alike follow the game, if not in
person, at least in spirit.

Q

Yachtsmen   In these times the Glasgow Nabob has turned
country squire for the summer months, and the
Clyde knows him only during "The Fortnight."
He owns a steam yacht, and his sons compete at
regattas in those sensitive little model racers
which Mr. Fife (like a skilful gardener) produces
in new varieties every year. At present the fashion
is all for the 23-footer, which will stand you in
anything between £300 and £500. Half a dozen of
these crafts may be made from the same design, and
the contests between them have a peculiar zest
since, with the racing machines identical in sail,
area, and construction, success depends entirely
upon skill. Besides the ordinary steam yacht and
the model racer, the Glasgow man of wealth favours
every kind of vessel, from the reformed torpedo
boat destroyer, which one of them possesses, to
the 65-ton cutter, which appears at every British
regatta, and among the latter class is the any-
weather boat in which the yachtsman of the old
school beats round Ireland or down to Spain. Our
Glasgow Nabob takes to yachting as his counterpart in less favoured places takes to the turf, and
his passion clears his eye and tans his face, and
gives employment to that mild and valiant person,
the yachting mariner. Also, as all admit who
have seen a Clyde regatta, it adds another beauty
to the Firth.

Even our city friend may, in a season of prosperity, turn practical yachtsman, and in his 5-ton
yawl may teach his boys the elements of maritime

skill—to abhor baggy sails as they should baggy trousers, to distinguish Loch Ridden from the Kyles on a misty day, and to avoid seeking anchorage in Loch Striven. They will learn to make Lamlash from Rothesay in two tacks with a south-east wind, to know the dangers of a west wind at Millport, and of a north-west in Rothesay Bay. They may even learn how one may enter that bay with one anchor and come away with two.

When his boys grow up they take unto themselves new friends, and the cottage by the loch will perhaps lose its charm; but the delight in white sails and salt water remains, and in the heyday of youth the flabby life of the English watering-place will never hold them long. As the lad sweats through the city summer, every wind that blows brings a new unrest, and when Saturday comes he will make off at one o'clock with the four others who share the five-rater with him, and in another hour you may see them scrambling aboard their boat in some quiet bay. Their yachting has a character; their vessel never seems dirty, their dinghy has her fenders. They never miss moorings nor lose their anchor, and even when the south wind dies and their boat swings like a pendulum in a sickening ground-swell off Arran, and the boom threatens every minute to break the crutches, and the sight of food brings the heart to the mouth, they remain as

A Friday to
Monday
calm and cool as ancient mariners of the oldest
school.

The Glennaquoich youth is a wise young
person. Yachting is more than cricket or golf or
tennis, for rain does not spoil his sport, and if
the sun is stronger than the wind, still is his boat
on the water and he a yachtsman with a weather
eye. And when the seas are up, and the trim
coast-line assumes a hard, barren look, he may toss
at anchor not unpleasantly, for a storm is not long
in spending itself in our lochs and archipelago.
A good Friday-to-Monday's yachting is something
straight from the gods. In the morning every
little coast hamlet flaunts its white flotilla to the
sun. Boat after boat puts out to join in the
chase, the low hulls drawing smoothly through
the water, and the bent heads of the crew, brown
and keen, beneath the towering white canvas.
However winds may veer, there is always a
course to be made, and the irregular configuration
of the Clyde and its lochs offers you endless
variety for your day's run. And if the weather
change, and you have to make for shelter, there
is safe anchorage in any of the little bays. When
the night comes, to lie on your back in a half-
decker at the moorings, watching drowsily the
lights of the town start up and disappear with
the pitching of your boat, until you sink to sleep
under the stars, is not the least of man's pleasures
here below.

Perhaps to something of the campaigning

character of this sport may be traced that rough- Yachting
ness which the wise men of the East have observed
in our manners; perhaps it is also responsible for
that heartiness which travellers have been good
enough to remark upon. At any rate,
yachting is the sport which counts here,
and its influence on the wellbeing of the
citizens may be introduced to the attention
of the sociologist.

VII

The Exhibition

TEN years after their last Exhibition the people Letter to
of Glasgow began to turn uneasily in their heavy editor
sleep of the provinces, and dreamed of enjoying
life in the open air, of spending summer evenings
in amusements less monotonous than listening to
volunteer bands. And, thirteen years after their
last one, comes this opportunity of acquaintance
with gracious things in life, to which formerly
they were strangers. This, far more than the
gigantic advertisement of manufactures, will be
the merit of the Exhibition. The costly apparatus
seems designed to obtain a more imposing result,
but, in truth, nothing short of it could have
produced the result at all. And it will be something if the people have pleasures strewn before
them, which are denied to them in ordinary
summers. Their lives will blossom like roses

in a desert place, and they who took their
pleasures dully will, with zest, enter into new
delights.   It must needs be that they will be

Russian Section

instructed also.   Machinery will teach them,
foreign contrivances will teach them, and colonial
produce will correct their ideas of climate.   But
the main lesson will be that their lives in other

[230]

years lacked charm and grace, and that, even Letter to editor without an Exhibition, the town could do much to afford them both. Bands need not always play " Reminiscences of ' San Toy,' " and the parks are there, needing only a very little of added attraction to make them compete (without chance of failure) with the flat monotony of Sauchiehall Street. Something was done when the close of the last Exhibition made a portentous blank in the life of the city. Music has been provided in the parks, and even garden chairs for the weary. But till now the open-air life was as far away as ever. Incoherent cries went up for kiosks at which one might take one's refreshment and one's ease in the open air. But no one heeded, and the heavy sleep of the provinces fell once more. No one could quarrel with the use to which the surplus from the Exhibition funds was put, for now our splendid collection of pictures has a suitable home. But when the next surplus is counted, let those in authority remember the greyness of life in the town ; let them arrange with the Town Council, which is the friend of man, to make the parks attractive on every night in summer. No lessee would take the risk of our climate ; let the holders of the surplus be bold and generous, and stake this money in the public interest. The parks are deserted in ordinary summers, save twice a week when a band plays in the evening for a couple of hours. Increase the bands, place here and there

a tea shop with a verandah, and a wonderful
change will be wrought. No one delights in
parading the streets for its own sake. One goes
to see and be seen, but one is shy of changing
the *venue*. Make the parks, by the simple means
of band and tea shop, as attractive as the Exhibition, and you will have done a good work. It
may be that you will have wrought a change in
the people's manners and habits, and will have
given them a new weapon to fight dulness with.
To put it on no higher ground, you will have
created a competitor with the public-house, and
no Town Councillor will ignore that obvious argument. And surely the surplus from a great
Exhibition of human industry would not be used
unworthily in making possible for human beings
lives that were more joyous and less destitute of
grace and charm.

VIII

Haunts

(1) George Square

George
Square THE Londoner who imagines he had turned his
back on his city's sins of arrangement finds them
repeated in every provincial town he comes to.
And so George Square is Trafalgar Square over
again—the same central monument, the same
weary desert of paving stones, the same feckless

designing of the spaces. The absence of the Land- George Square
seer lions may be counted to it as a negative
virtue, but the Scott monument is as dismal,
quite, as Nelson's. To set a "faithful portrait"
of a great writer on a pedestal eighty feet above
the street level, surely this is a form of strange
torture, survived from the Middle Ages. At the
head of a great column only a great symbol—a
great gesture—is permissible, although an emperor

standing guard over his realm might also be a
motive sufficiently dignified. But to hoist to this
height a man accustomed in life to walk the
streets like any other of us, one to whom close
observation of his fellows was a real daily need—
this offends against all that is just and appropriate. If it be retorted that the column and its
figure are the apotheosis of a great writer, why,

[233]

George Square — in the name of art, was the man not purged of his earthly look and transfigured into a great being, high over the land he made renowned? In cold weather, when we are snugly at home or in the Young Men's Christian Association Rooms, he is out in the cold and in danger, and this is the sole thought that the Scott monument stirs in us. It is no simple memorial of " sons to a father," as the Florentine monuments of the Renaissance were. Neither is it a symbol of enduring greatness. It is simply, like Nelson's, a man on the look-out tied to the mast-head. Burns's monument is better, because it is nearer the ground ; its clumsy, overgrown, earnest figure is truer to the man. Moreover, there is a faint touch of the appropriate in his standing here, for at a window at the south-east corner of the square his Bonnie Lass of Ballochmyle used to sit and see the folk go by when her poet was dead, and she no longer bonnie. But the square looks best when " a blast o' Janwar wind blaws hansel in on Robin," and brings with it snow. Then the stupid divisions of granolithic pavement from grass plots are blotted out, and the tramways run through lawns of snow, noiseless as sledges. And James Watt on his statue seems, indeed, a philosopher sunk in meditation, and as the snow settles on his head and lap, deeper and deeper seems his meditation. And Sir John Moore looks still and frozen, very like the hero of the ballad, " with his martial cloak around him." The Municipal Buildings, as

[234]

you view them from the Post Office portico, seem George Square
greatly, mysteriously official, like a façade in
Whitehall; the old hotels on the north side are
ever so far away, and the statues stand on their
white ground like chess-men on their board.

The windows of the General Post Office are
the Poor Man's Club. A man is staring out from
them, and sees not you, but a cotter's roof in
Morven, and a girl driving kye home at nightfall. An old mechanic ties up a well-thumbed
Weekly Mail, and addresses with a shaking,
laborious hand, and drops it among the foreign
newspapers, for his son, the engineer, in India.

(2) Queen Street Station

From the Post Office steps you see the station Queen Street
rise like a great yellow half-moon, and within Station
is cheery comfort, very welcome after snow or
rain. Nice brown trains are setting off to
England, others, less pleasant to look at, start for
more fascinating destinations—Fife, Inverness,
romantic spots in Scotland. At such a moment
one loses the sense (heavy enough at other times)
that Glasgow is a place cut off by its smoke and
grime from the Scotland that foreigners think of
when they figure us standing in kilts upon hills
" quite inaccessible " — Scott's " land of brown
heath and shaggy wood." It is not for nothing that
the railway has headquarters in Edinburgh and
goes by the Waverley route. It is the most
romantic station in Glasgow, and we can forgive

Queen Street Station its trains for being irregular, since they take us in the end to pleasant places. Buchanan Street Station is more ancient, but its romance is of the

North Side — George Square

embalmed, petrified, museum-like kind. And Queen Street is not romantic simply, but also agricultural. Something in the dear, old, comfortable,

[236]

unpretentious look of it tells you as much. It is more like a tavern—a battered caravanserai— than a station, its waiting-room quite like an inn-parlour, with space for four tolerably stout farmers, and a dark polished, mahogany table. There is passage, too, for a porter should he wish to bring coals, but he never does, and so the illusion of the inn-parlour is maintained. Out on the platform there is a spring of water, at which Ne'er Day people will mix their drink. Also there are benches, and this, may be, is why city people like to come here hours before their time, out of the rain, and discuss where the holi-day shall be spent. From the station, too, little parties of sightseers from the country set out, and hither they return long before their train will leave. Then "wee Maggies" and tired "Maws"—dazed wi' the lichts an' croods—may be settled on the benches with the "trumphery," and forgotten, what time the "Paws" are growing unco fu' and happy at a neighbouring public-house. What with whisky and fruit and newspapers, it provides more than any other place in the city for tired holiday-makers from the country. On feein' days the smell in it is richly of the soil, and many little scenes of yokel fun are enacted there, like the more decent passages in Teniers' pictures. The officials, if they ever wish to enforce decorum, remember that theirs is the Waverley route, and stay their hand. On market days the farmers

Queen Street Station may be traced from M'Coll's (where they have ended with apple dumpling) to the station by the hay-seed and corn samples fallen from their pockets.

To sum up, if romance ever brought the nine-fifteen to Glasgow it was into Queen Street Station. Just as the South-Western Company has appropriated Burns, the N.B. has laid claim to Sir Walter Scott (they may even have raised the neighbouring memorial to their protégé). The luckless Caledonian Railway has no man of genius except Sir James Thompson, who is already a director.

(3) Argyle Street

Argyle Street Argyle Street—together with Trongate, Queen Street Station, and part of Gallowgate—is " Gleska " to the country visitor—the place where are the waxworks, and the thieves, who, if you are not wary, steal your watch while you crane your neck to see the tops of the high buildings—the Polytechnic, where braws can be purchased much under cost price, and decent taverns that you enter through closes as into private houses. It is the scene of the traditional joke about Tonald and Angus from the Highlands, who waited all day in an entry " until all this procession went by, whateffer."

And it is not only our country friends who idle here, for Argyle Street is also the haunt of the loafer, the bookmaker, and that shabby, Argyle Street hopeful legion who gather in every city and wait

The Waxworks

on the turning up of things. At the same time it is the busiest street in the city. Here business cracks her stoutest whip, and men move fast and

Argyle Street silently and work very late. Every species of merchandise, from twopenny watches to cargoes of sugar, is sold in this district, and the buyers and sellers are ever on the pavement; and, besides these, there are debt-collectors and clerks out of collar making efforts to return to thraldom. You are jostled by Polish tailors running with hot-pressed clothes; little commission agents holding tight their black sample bags, which are their last straw to keep head above water; or perhaps some city Whittington, grey-locked and wiry, hurrying by with an undimmed eye fixed on the main chance. It is what you will—the saddest or merriest part of Glasgow. At night it is the Sauchiehall Street of a slightly poorer class. The lads and lasses of Gorbals and Gallowgate come daffing in crowds, chivying one another into the streets and up the entries, conducting their love-making by means of slaps and "dunches," and showing the Scots' self-consciousness that makes it so pathetically unspontaneous. If the nights are rainy, the young folk have either of the two "Wonderlands" or the "Brit." for their solace, and the street is deserted save for racing touts and hot-potato men. On Saturday night Argyle Street holds Saturnalia—not the "Continental Saturnalia" we hear so much about, but a time of squalid licence, when men stagger out of shuttered public-houses as out of a pit, and the street echoes to insane roaring and squabbles, to

[240]

the nerve collapse that ends a day's debauch of **Argyle Street** drink and football. On Sundays Argyle Street is a pleasanter place. The faithful pass to church, and the unregenerate make off to country places or to Paisley by the 'buses which start from opposite a vast, dull hotel, where ambassadors of commerce are breakfasting in brown rooms to the smell of O.K. sauce, while the brown landscapes by the late Horatio M'Culloch regard them from the walls. All day the street is a promenade, where the halflins sport their violet trousers and the girls their dresses of royal blue and magenta. All is peace and reconciliation, and the stains of the Saturday night fechts are washed away and forgotten.

It is a thronged, pulsating street at any time, more full of local character than any other in the city, and for a comprehension of Glasgow life the most essential. At one end the highway splits in two, and this circumstance must have offered a fine text in the old days for many a sermon. For the one way led to the Gallowsmuir, where criminals were hung, and the other is the London Road. Trongate, which is the east-end of Argyle Street, once upon a time contained the Glasgow Cross, and in it and its neighbourhood are situate what historical masonry Glasgow can boast. It was here the Tobacco Lords, in their great wigs and scarlet cloaks, strutted on their own appointed plainstanes in front of the Tontine—which **you**

R

Argyle Street may now see as a drapery warehouse, altered but little externally—and here rode the Adventurer at the head of his Highlandmen without stirring a single canny Glasgow heart, except, of course, Miss Walkinshaw's. Rob Roy, and that much more real person, Bailie Nicol Jarvie, and Defoe, and Dr. Johnson, and James Watt, and Tobias Smollett, and Robert Burns, and Walter Scott are among the figures you may conjure up as you tread the street to-day. And if you go back to older times for shadowy companions, there are Wallace, and Bishop Rae, and Queen Mary, and Oliver Cromwell.

(4) Buchanan Street

Buchana Street

Although Buchanan Street is in the middle of the city, it is, as I have said, our principal West-End promenade. Kelvinside being by day a man-deserted suburb, Great Western Road can never be a fashionable shopping street. Marketing may certainly be done among its butchers and bakers, but as it is not given to woman to shop alone, she comes to the city where her men-folk are, and in Buchanan Street there is prepared for her the best shops and a broad pavement whereon groups may gather and show that it is possible to converse without shouting, for the cars do not clatter down it, and its surface is of tar macadam. It is the only street in Glasgow where you can hear your own voice. It has, moreover, a real arcade that is more spacious and pretty than that of Burlington, shops that speak to the American heart in the tartans of old Gaul, tea shops more *bizarre* than Tokio's, a smoking room that is quite metropolitan, and a gorgeous furniture emporium where the actor-managers of the society plays at the Royalty view the unattain-

able for their scene in the Duke's Mansion. Thus Buchanan Street is a thronged place from twelve to four when the sun shines. It is the Princes Street of Glasgow, having, moreover, two sides as against the Edinburgh promenade, which, as every Glasgow man knows, is only " hauf a street." And further, it is a place paved with sentimental

Buchanan Street memories. The stucco goddesses that from their post at the Arcade front simper down upon the crowd could recall (if they had the mind) many a lovers' meeting held on the pavement at their feet. The stockbroker's clerk has long since commenced business for himself, and has married Miss So-and-So, of Hillhead, who used to meet him here at four o'clock of a fine afternoon. Now he has clerks of his own, is rather elderly, and she no longer slim, but they use the same trysting-place when now they plan at Christmas to take the children to a matinee at the pantomime. The street is the chief haunt of the strangers and tourists who find their way to the city, and there is abundance of trinkets and souvenirs in it for their attention. Also it contains everything that the Glasgow man of means requires in the leisure he allows himself. Here is the maker of guns and fishing tackle, the theatrical booking-office, the confidential cigar divan, the jeweller's where he can buy things as dear as anywhere else, the bookseller who sells the kind of literature you may read on the "Columba," and the tourist agencies with pictures of the Riviera and Norway, which shine by contrast with the greyness of Glasgow. Perhaps, of all these, the jewellers' shops are the most noticeable, and one cannot pass from Buchanan Street without stopping—as every one does—at "Edwards'." This is a most handsome shop, where Yachting cups, Swords of Honour, and boxes containing Freedoms of City

Bath Street

are displayed, and above its doorway is a great **Buchanan Street**
white clock, which marks the trysting-place of
the unromantic and sets the time to half the town.

Glasgow has no leisured class, but it has a leisure
hour, and if you wish to see her at her brightest,
pass along Gordon Street and down Buchanan
Street a little after noon. For an hour you may
see the tea-shop doors ever on the swing, and
young men sauntering arm-in-arm, and every one
gay and smiling, as if the day were Saturday.
But another hour and the street is half deserted,
and the office doors are clanging again. Buchanan
Street is the highway of Glasgow's leisure, and
you can stroll from top to bottom and back again
while you smoke one cigarette.

(5) Sauchiehall Street

Southerns will understand what manner of street **Sauchiehall Street**
this is if we tell them that Piccadilly (although
their Charing Cross is wrongly placed) is the
Sauchiehall Street of London. At the west end
of both are the parks and terraces, at the east end
the theatres. Our street has picture galleries like
the other—the Royal Institute, the Corporation
Galleries, and the rooms of the Royal Water Colour
Society; the shops, too, of the fashionable
milliners, haberdashers, Court photographers, book-
sellers, universal providers, dealers in old furniture,
and the necessary ladies' luncheon rooms at
Assafrey's and Skinner's. Moreover, it contains

Sauchiehall
Street

the Panorama, with Spatenbräu on draught and a
Morris-tube rifle range. It is the brightest and
gayest street in Glasgow, the only street of
pleasure. It has more painted buildings and gilded

Charing Cross
looking East

signs than any other, and its sky-line is more
irregular, piquant, and full of contrasts. At one
corner, where Wellington Street enters it, stands
a huge block of buildings for the sale and display

[246]

of " soft goods," at the other a row of little, two-
storey, suburban dwelling-houses, now given over
to photographers, with one-storey shops stocking
their former plots of pleasure-ground. The corner
of Wellington Street is a halting-place for the
tramways, and a great centre for shopping. The
English flower-girls that cry their wares in a
foreign tongue stand here, and here towards five
o'clock the first newsboys with the evening papers
arrive panting from the town. On the other side
of the street is the Wellington Arcade, and it is
at this point that the Piccadilly character of the
street for the moment fails. Perhaps the only
London touch in it is the German sausage shop
with the appetising still-life in the windows. For
the rest the Arcade is given over to third-class
businesses and faded toy shops that are a dim echo
of the Burlington Arcade. Across Renfrew Street
it is continued by the Queen's Arcade, a place of
trumpets (in brass), foreign stamps, scraps,
transfers, drawing slates, socialistic pamphlets, and
old books. At the other end it emerges on Cow-
caddens, which is a kind of Old Kent Road, and
at night is full of lights, and soldiers, and coster-
barrows, and working folk a-shopping. Through
the Wellington Arcade come the actors and
actresses from Garnethill (where the theatrical
birds of passage lodge) on their way to the theatres
or to the Hope Street Post Office, whence, in a
season of pantomime, principal boys in rustling
skirts send off remittances to their husbands in

Sauchiehall Street Queer Street. There is another arcade in the neighbourhood—the old, squat, red, ornamented one with the roof gone (taken, perhaps, by a creditor doing diligence) that blocks the head of Hope Street opposite to the Theatre Royal. A little shop in it belongs to a bagpipe maker, and here o' nights lonely Celts assemble to hear the wailing of the pipes. Between this roofless little court and Sauchiehall Street is a district inhabited by queer fellows—herbalists, Italian barbers (with the " Apotheosis of Victor Emmanuel " hanging on their walls), vendors of daring photographs and sporting papers, horse dealers, theatrical costumiers, and bookmakers from Flushing, who here " meet their old and new friends as per advertisement." From the little squalid lanes round the theatres down to the bright pubs. and shady supper-rooms of Sauchiehall Street it is the Soho of Glasgow.

(6) The West End

The West End It begins at Charing Cross, and with many interruptions extends nearly to Anniesland. It passes westwards along the Crescents, then over the splendidly crowned heights that look across the West End Park, northwards to Woodlands Road, then westwards to Gilmorehill, with the University and the streets about it, quiet as a cathedral close. Then from Byars Road westwards once more, and also northwards to Dowanhill and Kelvinside. And for all its name it is, for the

[248]

most part, as suburban as Streathamhill.   Even **The West End**
Pollokshields, which some suppose to be the
antipodes of Kelvinside, is in point of fact its
exact counterpart in an unfashionable district.
The terraces about Charing Cross and on the
heights above the park are certainly urban in
character, but the life in them is not different
from that of the suburbs.   In the morning
there is the same stream of men moving to
business in the city, in the evening the same
stream returning to home and dinner and comfort.
And in the interval, which is the whole day time,
there are the same nearly deserted streets, which,
but for ladies and children, would be entirely
lifeless. By day the West End of Glasgow is
Buchanan Street.   Yet the districts which compose the West End have little peculiarities of
their own.   Thus the Crescents, which are a
continuation of Sauchiehall Street, are inhabited
mainly by doctors, with here and there a school
for young ladies or for instruction in art, to leaven
the mass.   Woodside Crescent, which runs with
a splendid sweep up the hill from the Grand Hotel,
is the home of consulting physicians, as distinguished from others, while Woodlands Terrace,
which faces north, and is as dull as Great Stuart
Street in Edinburgh, is inhabited by those who
have not been fortunate enough to find houses
in Woodside Crescent.   The houses in Park
Terrace and Park Circus are mansions of the
wealthy, who live in affluence on the silver lining

The West End of the clouds that hang over Govan. Behind these houses, in streets that encircle the Free Church College, dwell prosperous families, loyal to the principles of Voluntaryism, and to names like John George for sons and Jane Mary for daughters. Of Dowanhill and Kelvinside, the

Great Western Road — Looking West

former is the more suburban. It is the quietest district imaginable, and its Nunnery does not seem out of place. The tramway cars do not run through it, and even the Subway, which in a manner serves it, does not come nearer than Byars Road. There are beautiful old villas in it, that sit among trees, and look grey and ancient,

and seem for generations to have been in the **The West End**
same families.   These are rare in Kelvinside,
which, because it is a newer district, is perhaps
more fashionable.   In place of trees you have
plots of *pro indiviso* pleasure-ground, with shrubs
and gravel walks, and instead of villas, rows upon
rows of ashlar-fronted, rubble-built houses, that
run along the Great Western Road until they are
headed off by the coal-pits and the Skaterigg
Co-operative Store and the Temple Gas Works.
This road is the pride of Kelvinside, and, until
the cyclists laid it waste, it deserved its praise.
On Sunday persons of fashion make the Church
Parade in it, and when they have gone home to
lunch, the Highland servant girls, with their lads
from the cross-channel boats or from the city
bars, come to let the observant person admire
the finest and healthiest human beings that the
town contains.   In the evening it is the pairing
ground for ordinary silent lovers, who sit on the
wall where the hedge shows a gap, and hold each
other's hands.   On Saturdays it is a place of
revelry, for where the houses end the Rugby
football fields adjoin it, and towards dusk on a
winter's afternoon you may see great streams of
men and girls returning home, and delighting, if
they have eyes, in the finest view which can be
had of the city.

(7) The Parks

The Parks   Of these the West End Park is the best for situation and popularity of character. It touches almost every kind of district in the city; the University and Park Terrace look across it from different points to Overnewton and Finnieston. And as it is central, it is also a thoroughfare. Its gates are never shut, and all kinds of people pass through, and yet by day it has no great life of its own. Students pass through in droves on their way to the University, and business men go through it of a morning on their way to their offices, but for the rest it is mostly given over to disabled workmen, who sun themselves in the summer-house and spin little tame discussions that lead to nothing. Sometimes old whales and barnacles that once were in the coasting trade join them, and tell of salvage services which, if the tow-rope had held, would have made shipowners of the narrators. On the high ground at the flagstaff you may see nursemaids with valuable babies from Park Terrace, but they do not venture often into the plains. The Botanic Gardens are pure West End, for Kelvinside encompasses them behind and before. They are not open at night, and except on Saturdays and Sundays are not greatly used in the daytime by passers through. But they are a happy hunting ground for nursemaids, who come here to air their charges and collogue with the ranger and the policeman; and sometimes dear old ladies **The Parks** come, who sniff the sunshine through black veils, and are for ever fumbling in satchels for scent bottles and old letters, although (if the season permits) crocuses are gleaming in the lawns and hawthorns are budding and the good odour of spring is in the air. At their mid-day meal hour house-painters dauner in from their work close

by, and smoke pipes and discover benches where greasy newspapers may be smoothed out and read. The place is famous for its flower-beds and trees and lawns and conservatories. It contains the "hanging woods of Kelvin," where wild flowers grow and visitors are requested to keep off the blue-bells. It is the favourite park of the Corporation, and it is handsomely treated. Here

The Parks is the best bandstand in the city, and of a summer night the Glasgow Male Voice Choir sing songs that, if one may say so, reach every heart within earshot. Here, too, the Corporation have provided garden seats, on which, for one penny, you may take your dolorous ease what time your heart is being reached. On the south side of the Clyde is the South Side Park, with the finest approach (by a flight of steps) of any in the city. From the foot of the flagstaff the view is so free and fine that every year some one declares in the papers that he saw Ben Nevis, while a cloud of witnesses, better informed, next day assure him that he saw nothing of the kind. Also on the South Side is the beautiful old formal garden of Camphill, finely preserved, with its orchard and Italian cypress trees and boxwood borders. In the East End there is the Alexandra Park, with a hazardless golf course, and a boat pond on which grandfeyther frae Crown Street teaches Alick's yin what Shamrock II. must do to win the cup. It is also the place in which juvenile football clubs meet to settle matches which are only less important than internationals. The ancient Green of Glasgow is become its Hyde Park, in which Socialists and advanced people argue about the Existence and Nature of Chance and Luck (so-called), or about the old problem of the Hen and Egg. May Day and Labour demonstrations are held in this same park, on which Prince Charlie reviewed the adherents to another lost cause.

The most human thing that the parks can show is Children's Day, which is held on a Saturday in spring.   There is a procession of children, ranked according to schools, with banners and music, and in the parks there are games and very light refreshment at the Corporation charges, and singing and more music.

The Ballade of James Hamilton Muir

to his Friends:

BEING A LAMENT ON THE TERMINATION

OF AN

ADVENTURE ON THE HIGH-SEAS

OF LITERATURE.

. . .

NEW YEAR'S DAY, 1902.

The Ballade of James Hamilton Muir to his Friends *is reprinted here from a leaflet in the collection of Sylvester Bone. It claims that* Glasgow in 1901 *was no money-spinner, but it was certainly successful and well-reviewed, and was selling well in its second printing at the time the* Lament *was issued.*

I.

Struck are the Colours from the Mast,
  The tattered Sails thrash to and fro,
The splendid Frigate's day is past,
  The New Year takes the Old in tow.
Farewell, old Ship, farewell the Show
  Thou bravely mad'st beneath the Sun.
Over the Side we now must go,
  We who WERE Muir in Nineteen One.

II.

As Mariners we once were classed,
  Superbly fit to yeave and yo;
The salt Sea-Quid did break our Fast,
  The Puffin-Bird sang high, sang low.
The lone Sea-Furrow we did sow
  And reaped it on the Homeward Run;
Oh! how the good TRADE Winds did blow
  When WE were Muir in Nineteen One.

III.

The Gaff is blown, and now:—'Avast
  Rolling the Logs, that lie a-row!'
Back is the Cobbler to his Last,
  Back is the Baker to his Dough
(Valhalla flits to Jericho).
  Our Woof is Warped, our Yarn is Spun.
Man, vaunt but little here below—
  Lo! we were MUIR in Nineteen One!

ENVOY.

Critics, our Gain you wish to know
  For this great Work that we have done?
A Friend or two and a Guinea or So—
WHEN WE WERE MUIR IN NINETEEN ONE.

                                    J.H.M.

INDEX